Navigating the 'N' Word

How Keeping "Niggas" Alive is Killing Black Folk

Navigating the 'N' Word

How Keeping "Niggas" Alive is Killing Black Folk

Brady Goodwin Jr.

The 3rd book in the MORE-ality series
Connecting Hip Hop to History and the Here-after

Self-Published through Urbanremixproject.com

Navigating the "N" Word: How Keeping "Niggas" Alive is Killing Black Folk

Self-Published by Brady Goodwin Jr through
Urbanremixproject.com
Philadelphia, PA

Printed in the United States of America by Createspace
Cover design: Jamel Rashad

Edited by: Donna Wyche

Dedicated to *ALL* the descendants of Africans in America

Table of Contents

Foreword: Navigating the Course of Culture.................. vii

1 Navigating the Power of Naming.. 1

2 Navigating the Power of Resurrection 21

3 Navigating the Strength of Street Knowledge............43

4 Navigating the Strength of Street Knowledge (Part 2)
....67

5 Navigating the Strength of Strawman Arguments....89

6 Navigating the Highs and Lows of Hierarchy 109

7 Navigating the Highs and Lows of Hierarchy (Part 2)
.... 131

Appendix: Navigating the 'B' Word 157

Foreword: Navigating the Course of Culture

How does culture work? Many people have a difficult time answering this question. Instinctively, they know *that* it works; but many are not sure how or why it works. Some would go as far as to assert that, even though culture works for others, it does not work for them. "I am my own individual" they might say. "I'm not the product of any culture," they'll add. Everyone wants to be the exception but to a large degree, we are all the products of culture. As the world shrinks through technology and globalization, we are, increasingly, becoming the products of a multiplicity of cultures as we pick and choose various artifacts from different cultures to embrace as part of our own identity.

There are some cultural artifacts which might have worked well in their original context, but which work much differently when transferred into new cultures. Sometimes the difference is better and sometimes it is worse. There are other cultural items that, when closely scrutinized, do not even work well in their original contexts. This book will look at the word "nigger" and seek to answer the question, 'which of these is the case: is it a word that works better or worse now than it did in its original context?' Before we get there, let's take a look at culture and how it works.

This book is the third in a series on what I call *MORE*-ality – maximizing the potential for good through the integration of faith and culture. In the first book of the series (*The Death of Hip Hop, Marriage & Morals*) I introduced the following definition, along with the Eight Pillars of Culture. Please familiarize yourself with this definition and the eight pillars (below) as they will be helpful in understanding and interacting with the remainder of this book.

Culture is the way a group of people comes together to answer life's questions. From one culture to the next, the answers might change but the questions remain the same. These questions (and their answers) form the eight pillars of culture. They are:

1. **Food** (What to eat and how to prepare it, serve it, eat it?)
2. **Fashion** (How to protect the body from adverse elements and unauthorized eyes?)

3. **Dialect** (How do we make communication easier for those in our group while keeping outsiders at bay?)

4. **Art** (What ideas, events and emotions are worth reproducing? And how skillfully/uniquely can this be done?)

5. **Values** (How do we preserve, perpetuate and progress our way of life?...e.g. technology, economy, dating, mating, law and government)

6. **Ultimate Questions** (What is our Origin? Destiny? Meaning? And how do we know?)

7. **Heroes** (Who among us, living or dead, has helped to answer these questions most?)

8. **Historic Events** (What are the memorable moments when these questions were answered for us? e.g. Holidays)

The Death of Hip Hop, Marriage & Morals focused on *values*. The second book in this series, *From Hip Hop to Hollywood: The Art of Christianity* dealt with *art*. Both books sought to communicate the idea that it is the question of *values* which ties the eight pillars together. If a culture has poor answers to the *values* question or, is not trying to answer the *values* question while answering the question of *art* or *food* or, in the case of this book, *dialect*, then that culture will soon unravel from within or be exploited and depleted from without. (For a more thorough discussion on this, see chapter four of *The Death of Hip Hop, Marriage & Morals*)

Look at the cultural question associated with dialect (the third pillar). In the case of the word "nigger," it must be admitted that it performs this function very well in the black community. With all the ways the 'N' word can be used from one African American to another, it allows those within the community to easily communicate a variety of possible meanings while mystifying those outside of the culture. Not only that, but since the late 1960s, those outside of the culture have been banned from using the word publically without suffering the social backlash of having done so. For this reason, many people of color take pride in the word, believing that blacks have confiscated it, or better yet, have commandeered it from whites in order that it might serve a new and better purpose.

However, this is not the only pillar that the word must satisfy. Remember that culture is held together by the *values* questions. And, if *values* is detached from a particular culture's *dialect*, then those within that culture might find that while they are working to keep certain words alive, those same words are working towards the death and demise of those who use them.

This book in no way aims to communicate the idea that the manifold problems facing African Americans today are all the result of the continued use of one word and that, if we could ban that word, the dark clouds would roll away and the sun would shine into the social and political world of black people in this nation. No— for it is not mere words that have injured black people but rather, racist and classist actions and ideas. But what are words if not containers for ideas? Words can be positive or negative depending on the ideas they carry and convey. Thus, even though words themselves cannot do any harm, if one embraces the negative ideas behind a particular word, this can add present-day insult to historical injury. On top of this, it is because the ideas behind certain words are still very much alive that the words themselves die hard. And it might be that the only way to challenge the negative ideas which lead to the negative actions is to challenge the containers which carry the idea, i.e. to challenge and reject the word.

Therefore, by looking at the ways in which the 'N' word has functioned in the past, and the attempts that have been made to do away with it, as well as its resurfacing in modern Hip Hop culture, this book will challenge the idea that the word has been commandeered in order to perform an entirely new function. It will be demonstrated that, at the street level, the word performs very much of the same function for which it was originally summoned in the first place in its original context – on the lips of American masters of African slaves, and that is so precisely because it still carries very much of the same idea now as it did then.

1

Navigating the Power of Naming

What do you do when you hear the word "Nigger?" Do you cringe? Does it depend on who is around? Does it depend on who is saying it and what is the context? Or perhaps it depends on the way the word is being used. Does it seem like hypocrisy or does it make perfect sense to you that blacks should be able to use the word but not whites? Maybe you have been looking for a way to start a conversation about the word with your black friend, your white friend, your peers, your youth or elders but you just don't know what to say or where to begin? After reading this book, you will be fully equipped to engage in a modern discussion on this age-old topic.

There is no doubt that, of all of the debated words in the history of the English language, "Nigger" is the most hotly disputed. It is so emotionally charged that, publically, we have reduced it to an initial—the 'N' word. In private, however, it is not the first letter but the last which is debated. Does the word end in 'er' or simply with an 'a'? Furthermore, does the 'a' ending change the word's meaning into something desirable or, at least, acceptable? And if so, why is it that whites are still banned from saying it, even with the new ending? Lastly, the question is, should the word be banned for blacks as well or should it be preserved for posterity in order to highlight the history of an oppressed people who overcame?

Those who would retain the word take a certain pride in having wrestled it away from whites who can no longer wield it publically without backlash. Only blacks can say it and when they do, it no longer carries any of the negativity originally meant by whites. Blacks have taken one of the instruments of their oppression and now wear it as an emblem of their freedom. But others have asked, is this even possible?

It should be remembered that this would not be the first time in history when a term or symbol of derision and defeat has been reversed by those who were meant to be tormented by it. In his 1995 song, "The Truth" Conscious rapper KRS One posed the question to modern-day Christians asking how they could joyfully wear a cross as an ornament around their necks. After all, wasn't the founder of Christianity, Jesus, publically executed by being nailed to a cross and left to die? KRS One further asks

> What if Jesus Christ, was hung upon a tree/ Upon every church wall this is what you'd see/ If Jesus Christ was shot in the head with no respect/ We'd all have little gold guns around our neck/ If Jesus Christ was killed in an electric chair, now get it/ You'd be kneeling to the electric chair with Jesus still in it

This, to him, seemed like lunacy. But the Christian's response was simple: the cross of Christ, while for a short time meant his death and defeat, was soon turned into a symbol of life and victory by Jesus' resurrection from the dead. The instrument that should have spelled "the end" of Christianity was really the beginning of it all! KRS One's point is an excellent one only if there is no resurrection to speak of.

What's more, the very term "Christians" (literally meaning "little Christs") was originally meant as a dis to those who believed that Jesus was the Jewish Messiah, the Christ. But Jesus' followers soon embraced and began proudly using the term that was meant to belittle them. This was their way of proclaiming, "We are glad to be considered smaller versions of this great individual." The term which was meant to only have negative connotations was reversed so that it only had a positive meaning for those within the group being labeled. We can ask, 'is what has happened with the word "nigger" similar to either of these examples?'

Or, perhaps the word functions like a very different kind of historic relic, one that could not be turned into a symbol of hope or love. Jewish men and women today would not dream of taking a symbol, such as the Nazi swastika and attempting to use it positively within their own communities. Whenever the logo is displayed it is immediately met with disgust and contempt. Those who were more militant among the Jewish people have adopted the slogan "Never Again," vowing to never allow anyone to make them feel threatened with what they faced in the past in the Holocaust.

African Americans are familiar with this type of reaction to symbols. A noose hanging from a tree or a Confederate flag atop a pole will bring about a similar reaction as the swastika to an Israeli. The original meaning behind each of these symbols registers as too hurtful, too hateful, to ever be changed or invested with goodness. The question is raised, 'does the 'N' word fit better in this category?' Is it too inherently evil to ever be redeemed? Or does it belong with the former examples, functioning much like Jesus' cross? In the miraculous resurrection story of African American culture and life, does the continued use of the 'N' word by blacks now reflect how these resilient people have overcome? Has the word which was once used to slander and slay the souls of black folk become a source of their virtue and vitality, just like the term "Christians" did for early followers of Jesus?

This last question must be answered in the negative. For in the case of Jesus' early followers, the term which was meant to deride and dismiss them was changed in their dialect to only encourage them to follow Jesus with undying pride and devotion. Its connotation was, for them, never a negative thing. However, the 'N' word, even with all of its possible meanings and spellings, often still carries the sting which was originally intended by those who saw nothing positive or valuable in the word or in the people to whom it was applied. But there is a reason why many African Americans would like to keep the word alive. The word itself has no inherent power. What does have extreme power is the process in which the word has been involved – i.e. the naming process.

The Power of Naming

It might be hard to find an individual, in this day and age, who knows what his or her name actually means. The mind rushes to think of the young, urban female with her beautifully exotic, multisyllabic name; a name too recently invented by her parents to bear any historical significance. But this was not always the case and in some cultures around the world, the ancient naming traditions still continue. In these communities a name is important because it symbolizes what the birth of the child means to the family's legacy, to society or even to the world. In some African cultures children are named according to their birth order. In other cultures children are named after ancestors or rulers of the past.

Still in others, children are named according to what the parents believe the child's destiny to be – the baby's name tells the world why he or she has been sent here.

Even in America, a typical baby-naming book will inform parents that choosing the perfect baby name is one of the most important things a parent can do because the child's name will define the kind of life he or she will have. In light of this, parents are told that names should be easy to spell, easy to pronounce, pair well with the child's last name and not invite bullying. All of this forethought is necessary because parents have the power and right to call their children something that will follow them (and hopefully guide them) for the rest of their lives.

Naming is not just a parental right. It is a leadership trait as well. Good leaders are often re-naming the individuals around them in light of outstanding qualities they observe in a person. Sadly, bullies use this leadership quality in the most negative way when they give unflattering nick-names to their victims based on a person's foibles and imperfections. When one considers the matter further, there might even be a spiritual aspect of the naming process. The man who led the twelve disciples who changed the world, Jesus, was good at giving new names to his followers after they exhibited some winsome quality or another. In fact, in the biblical narrative recorded in Genesis, one of the first things God does, after making the first man, is to delegate some of his own authority to the man by tasking him with the job of naming all of the animals.

It can be powerful, parental, and even God-like, to engage in the process of naming a person. But what kind of power must one hold in order to name not just another person, but an entire race of people? And what if, while wielding such awesome power, the one doing the naming has no intention of branding people with a label that praises their ability and potential but instead focuses on one particular trait belonging to that people? The particular trait, in this case, is their skin color. And not their true skin color with all of the wonderful gradations of rich, dark African skin – but, a hyperbolic caricature of that skin. This group of people is so dark, they might as well be Negro...Black! And the prevailing attitude is not that black is beautiful. No, black is, at best, pitiable; and at worse, pitiful. This is the same power of naming that a bully exercises on his victims. He simply picks one feature that is perceived to be a flaw and then turns it into a title which supposedly says all that is worth knowing about the individual. "Neger!" "Negro!" "Nigra!" "Nigger!" "Black!" That is what you are. That is all you are.

This God-like naming of an entire race is the intoxicating power that whites have been drunk with for several hundred years. For if it was indeed an act of God that made man, it will take no less than a god to unmake men. Whites assumed this divine authority, not in order to enrich Africans. Rather, they used it and the name "nigger" to strip them of their dignity and humanity. And once people have been dehumanized, there is no longer any responsibility associated with treating them as less than human. This is why it is common for victims to be called dehumanizing words and names while being physically or sexually assaulted. The ones inflicting harm must, somehow, convince themselves that their actions are not being done to another human-being, but rather, to something less than human.

Of course, after long centuries, conscience, common-sense reasoning and Christianity finally combined to convince enough white Americans in the northern United States that Africans were indeed human beings and that they should no longer be used as slave labor. The Civil War compelled southern whites to respect that sentiment and then, the Civil Rights Movement challenged segregation, the system that took the place of slavery as a way to continue to treat blacks like "niggers." One of the great successes of that movement is that it sensitized a nation of whites to the plight of blacks in America; to understand that these were indeed human beings whom dogs were being unleashed upon; whom fire hoses were being opened against; and whose rights were being denied. Seeing this, many began to come to terms with the fact that the name "nigger" was not appropriate for this resilient people, full of so much self-respect.

To continue to call blacks "niggers" whites would have to forget about Jessie Owens destroying Hitler's myth of Aryan supremacy at the 1936 Summer Olympics in Berlin. They would have to forget about the artistic creations and innovations of the Harlem Renaissance and the great many inventions given to the world by the industrious minds and hands of African American craftsmen. They would have to forget about the patient determination with which blacks marched and legislated in order to have their constitutional rights recognized at the local level. And as much as some might try to forget these things, none could forget how the Civil Rights Movement gave way to the Black Power Movement of the mid to late 1960's, when a new generation of African American youth had been emboldened to resist the system and reject the status quo, even if it meant resorting to not so peaceful protests.

It was the Black Power Movement that effectively ripped the 'N' word away from whites. This was not just because militant young blacks threatened to stand up for themselves by any means necessary. It was more because eloquent young blacks embraced the "black is beautiful" ideas of men like Malcolm X who advocated the need for "Black self-love." In his famed 1964 speech "The Ballot or the Bullet" Minister Malcolm taught, "We have to change our own mind. You can't change [the white man's] mind about us. We've got to change our own mind about each other. We have to see each other with new eyes."

Heavily influenced by the writings of Malcolm X was Stokely Carmichael. After having begun in the non-violent movement, Carmichael eventually abandoned the philosophy of Martin Luther King and rose to head the more militant Black Panther Party. For him, seeing each other "with new eyes" did not mean that blacks could no longer be niggers. Rather, it meant that blacks could no longer be niggers in the way that whites meant it. Everyone to whom the word was applied must now be viewed in a completely different way. What was important was not that what black people were called was changed, but what was meant when they were called. In an historic encounter with police (while standing alongside Dr. Martin Luther King in 1966) Carmichael used the term "Black Power" for the first time in the media as he warned, "You tell them white folks in Mississippi that all of the scared niggers are dead."[1] The implication was two-fold: There are niggers who are still alive and well; and these niggers are not the scared ones that southern whites were used to!

This, again, is the power of naming but working with a kind of centrifugal force. The name that whites had given blacks no longer meant the negative thing that it once meant and whites can no longer use it. Why? Because blacks now mean something completely different by it. By changing the meaning of "nigger," they have in effect renamed themselves and breathed new hope into their destiny. All the niggers who could be scared off and killed off have already been so. But for those who remain, the term must now mean "survivor" and soon "overcomer"; it refers to the ones who were not supposed to be able to make it, but did. Therefore the word was embraced ironically, rhetorically even.

This rhetorical reversal of the terminology was not unique to Stokely Carmichael. African Americans have a history of investing negative words with positive ideas. Often, this was all that a people who were used to being viewed negatively could do in order to retain some sense of their own positively human nature. Professor and author, Judson L. Jeffries, while writing on Black Panther Party leader Huey P. Newton, chronicled the way in which the word "bad" came to mean "good" in African American circles. He writes that it

> Can be traced back to slavery. John Little, a fugitive slave who escaped to Canada, once recalled that Southern whites seeing a black man in shackles would often say, "Boy, what have you got those on for? . . . if you weren't such a bad nigger you wouldn't have them on." "Bad niggers" were viewed by white slaveholders and those who supported the institution of slavery as slaves who were dangerous and difficult to control. However, for blacks, the individual in question was one who refused to submit and was willing to fight the system. Hence, other slaves generally admired these individuals. To be perceived as a "bad nigger," then as well as now, is nothing less than a badge of honor in the black community.[2]

What whites considered negative was, for blacks, a very good and courageous thing. This opposite-ethical dynamic has continued right up to the modern day and has been enshrined in early Hip Hop culture. In the

1980s, legendary rap group Run DMC lyrically clarified that when they said "bad" they meant, "Not bad meaning bad but bad meaning good!" In the following chapters we will see how the dynamic of the "bad nigger" has played out in history.

Black Panther Party leader Eldridge Cleaver once referred to the party's founder, Huey P. Newton, as "the baddest motherf*cker who ever set foot inside of history." He, of course, meant this as a high compliment. The party embraced the reversed meaning of the adjective "bad." But when it came to attaching it to the noun "nigger," the same semantic spin did not always immediately apply. Like Run DMC, "bad nigger" could be "bad meaning good," but it could also be "bad meaning bad." Consider the conversation Black Panther Party chairman Bobby Seale had with his wife concerning the naming of his son, recorded in 1968[3]

> When my wife Artie had a baby boy, I said, "The nigger's name is Malik Nkrumah Stagolee Seale."
>
> "I don't want him named that!" Artie said.
>
> I had read all that book history about Stagolee, that black folkloric history, because I was hung up on that stuff at the time, so I said, "Malik Nkrumah Stagolee Seale!"
>
> "Why Stagolee?" Artie asked.
>
> "Because Stagolee was a bad nigger off the block and didn't take sh*t from nobody. All you had to do was organize him, like Malcolm X, make him politically conscious. All we have to do is organize a state, like Nkrumah attempted to do." Nkrumah was a bad motherf*cker and Malcolm X was a bad nigger. Huey P.

Newton showed me the nigger on the block was ten motherf*ckers when politically educated, and if you got him organized. I said, "Stagolee, put Stagolee on his name," because Stagolee was an unorganized nigger, to me, like a brother on the block. I related to Huey P. Newton because Huey was fighting niggers on the block. Huey was a nigger that came along and he incorporated Malcolm X, he incorporated Stagolee, he incorporated Nkrumah, all of them.

Thus, during this period as African Americans were rebranding themselves through the process of naming, the word "nigger," at the very least, spoke to the potential of the average black person to become conscious, educated and organized, and therefore, dangerous to the system (bad meaning good) instead of being prison-bound on the block, and dangerous to other blacks (bad meaning bad).

The Power of Shaming

But even on colored lips, the word still had the potential to sting like the crack of a slave-master's whip. This is because blacks did not always, only mean the beautiful thing that Stokely Carmichael or Bobby Seale might have meant when they referred to their own people as "niggers." Since the 1970's, this busy little word has performed double duty in the African American community. Not only has it been used rhetorically to point out the irony that the ones who were seen as worthless and sub-human had constantly proven their inestimable worth and humanity. But it has also been used by African Americans to explain the uncivilized actions of some members of the race who fail to live up to their potential; those who live as if the old definition was an accurate one. The word "nigger" is used to shame these individuals into conforming to more socially acceptable, community empowering behavior.

Author and visual artist Naeem Mohaiemen sees that it was the artistic work of the black radical group The Last Poets, particularly, their 1970 piece, "Niggers Are Scared of the Revolution" which started the "reappropriation" of the 'N' word by blacks and paved the way for its later "over-usage" in Hip Hop music.[4] He quotes these lyrics from The Last Poets to illustrate how they commandeered the word:

> Niggers are scared of revolution but niggers shouldn't be scared of revolution because revolution is nothing but change, and all niggers do is change. Niggers come in from work and change into pimping clothes to hit the street and make some quick change. Niggers change their hair from black to red to blond and hope like hell their looks will change.

One can see a similarity between this poetic discourse and modern, popular rap music but the connection is not as direct as Mohaiemon suggests. It will be shown in chapters three through six that when Hip Hop began in the mid-1970s, it resisted the 'N' word for close to thirteen years; almost a full twenty years after "Niggers Are Scared of the Revolution." So there must be some other historical development which accounts for Hip Hop's eventual embracing of the word. Also, as seen from the Bobby Seale quotation above, the word "nigger" was a part of the dialect, at least, for members of the Black Panther Party, already for several years before this 1970 artistic piece. Nonetheless, Mohaiemon is helpful on this point: through artistic works like "Niggers Are Scared of the Revolution," the shaming power of the 'N' word was harnessed by members of the Black Power Movement during this time in order to goad African Americans into action. To this day, blacks continue to tap in to the 'N' word for its shaming potential.

An interesting example of this occurred in 2015 when a white, South Carolina judge found himself in hot water for using the offensive word. Judge James B. Gosnell Jr. was selected to serve in the racially charged case of a young, white male who had murdered nine African Americans during a mid-week Bible-study at a South Carolina church. But right after Gosnell was selected, it was discovered that he had been reprimanded back in 2003 for using the 'N' word in court. "There are four kinds of people in the world," Gosnell had told a young black defendant. "There are black people, white people, rednecks, and niggers."

One might wonder how a judge could continue to serve for twelve years after making such a controversial statement from the bench. Was this just a reflection of the south's lingering racism? After all, it was only after protests erupted in the wake of the church shooting that the confederate flag was finally removed from the nearby state capital building. But the judge had a different excuse for his unprofessional conduct. It turns out that Gosnell was only repeating what he had heard spoken by an African American sheriff's deputy. The judge's intention was to motivate the young black defendant to change his life by shaming him out of behaving in a way that would cause others to classify him as a "nigger."

The words Judge Gosnell borrowed from this sheriff's deputy show that while blacks may mean no harm when referring to themselves ironically as "niggers," it is also common to use the word in a derogatory way when aiming to shame other blacks out of acting undignified. In using the word this way, what remains unaddressed is the social reality that, often, whites get the benefit of the doubt and are innocent until proven guilty of being rednecks, while historically, blacks have been presumed guilty of being niggers and must prove (or improve) themselves until they are finally innocent of the charge. With the name, comes the shame.

In 2015, Hannibal Burress, (the comedian who is credited with bringing the misdeeds of American icon Bill Cosby to light during a 2014 comedy set) made another attempt at social commentary when he jokingly asked, why the National Association for the Advancement of Colored People (NAACP) was still using the phrase "colored people." After all, "black" is the way African Americans are most commonly referred to today. But "black" does not have the same kind of historical significance as the term Burress believes to be outdated.

As early as 1903, NAACP cofounder and scholar W.E.B. Du Bois chronicled the reason why both words are important in the phrase "colored people"; reasons that might still hold true today. He recounts that, just before the time of the Civil War, northern blacks were inspired by mulatto immigrants from the West Indies who differentiated between themselves and slaves. In this, northern blacks saw an avenue toward racial equality. They joined forces with these individual to demand full suffrage, not as "Negroes" but, as people of color.[5] While this seemed to overlook the plight of southern blacks, this new term stressed, on one hand, the reality of the vast diversity in the complexion of brown-skinned individuals and, on the other hand, the humanity of these individuals. They demanded to be seen as people first, and *then*, people of color second. Though it has become customary to use the term "black" to refer to people of color, particularly those of African descent, it is worth noting that the phrase "colored people" was one of the first attempts by blacks to take the power of naming onto their own tongues for a change and it was original in its time.

Those who wish to retain the 'N' word in order to positively redefine it and use it to rename the black race will have to acknowledge that it carries a powerful shaming effect like no other alternative word or phrase. In all these years, it has proven to be impossible to keep the word alive without also preserving its ability to kill the self-esteem of those to whom it is applied. Like the precious ring in J. R. R. Tolken's *The Lord of the Ring* trilogy, it was created to rule over others and deemed so powerfully destructive that it must be destroyed. Yet all those who volunteered to carry it and vowed to do away with its evil intent found that its corrupting influence was too great. The ring they sought to destroy ended up destroying them. Only the hobbit Frodo Baggins was able to resist the ring's lure long enough; to deny his own desire to use it in order to lord over others; and to successfully carry it to its place of destruction. Sadly, as was the case in the film series, the same is true in real life—there are no black hobbits. Therefore, this book will look at several young, black would-be "Frodos," some seeking to carry the 'N' word to its death, while others seeking to use its naming powers, only for good. And in each case, we will assess their efforts to successfully navigate the word's destructive force.

Those who wish to retain the 'N' word in order to shame members of the black race into acting more "dignified" must recognize that it is a powerful thing to name another person. The names we give people greatly impact how we see and treat them as well as how they see themselves and allow others to treat them. It also impacts the way we see ourselves if we believe that we have the power to label people with a name that dehumanizes them. In this, we overestimate ourselves and underestimate our fellow man, as did the originators of the term "nigger."

Lastly, those who wish to do away with the word must reckon with the fact that it is extremely hard to kill a word. In fact, with this particular word, most have ceased trying because of the difficulty involved. Unlike Jesus Christ who claimed to have resurrection power within himself, the 'N' word makes no such claims and has no such ability.[6] And yet, as often as it has been laid to rest, the word has been raised back to life. The next chapter will observe the word's seeming power of resurrection.

2

Navigating the Power of Resurrection

On July 9th, 2007, thousands of people gathered in the streets of Detroit for what promised to be a historic event. The day saw many festivities, including beautiful, black women dressed in native garb performing African dance while strong black men beat African drums in the middle of the blocked off roadway. However the most eye-catching display was the large casket being pulled down the city corridor by a pair of horses. As it turned out, this grand event was a funeral. But who or what lay within the massive coffin? Was it a person? Sort of. But more than that, it was a persona. A personification, actually. An idea embodied in a word; in *that* word. This was touted as a "Funeral for the 'N' Word."

The event was put together by the NAACP as a symbolic statement that it was time for African Americans to bury the nasty name in the past in order to clear the way for a stigma-free future. The casket, draped with artificial black roses, was taken to Detroit Memorial Park Cemetery where it was buried. Similar, simultaneous events were held in other cities around the country that day. The 'N' word was never to be heard from again; that is, until one turned on the radio to hear the latest rap song proudly promoting its continued use. If the 'N' word died on July 9th, 2007, it was immediately resurrected.

When asked about the "Death of the 'N' Word", Hip Hop mogul Russell Simmons said that he supported a voluntary ban of the word but would not dream of trying to make it mandatory. Rappers "can use it," he said, because it is "their job to create accurate portrayals of society."[7] But just what is it that rappers are accurately depicting when they speak of "niggas" in society? Are they simply telling America about the lifestyles of people who have been "branded" with the 'N' word? Or, are they saying that their lyrics do, in fact, come from and speak about actual niggas? Either way, the NAACP's attempt to put the word in the ground was short lived because the Hip Hop generation had gotten hold of the word's duel power – the power of naming and the power of shaming. Perhaps in time, the Hip Hop generation will learn what the Civil Rights generation was ready to memorialize at the funeral for the 'N' word, i.e. that this dual power is too much to manage and it cannot be controlled.

This 2007 funeral was not the first time that African Americans endeavored to put the 'N' word to death. Way before Hip Hop took hold of it; even before the Black Power Movement got its tongue around it, back in 1963, African American author and activist James Baldwin attempted to put an end to the 'N' word by changing, not its definition, but rather, its referent – the one to whom the term was applied. His was a creative method for putting a twist on the twisted name.

In the documentary *Take this Hammer*, Baldwin expresses his belief that what you invent, what you feel the need to create, reveals who you really are. He sees creation as simply "a form of self-expression." He reasons from this that white Americans have felt the need to create and keep alive this idea of a "nigger." But, Baldwin says, he has always known that he is not a nigger. He explains to whites watching the program, "What you were describing and what you were afraid of [was] not me. *You* invented it. It had to be something you were afraid of [and] you invested me with." Pulling all of this logic together, Baldwin put his spin on the word when he alleged, "If I am not the nigger, and if it is true that your invention reveals you . . . then who is the nigger? I give you your problem back . . . you're the nigger, baby. It isn't me."

This took the power of naming and the use of centrifugal force to another level. Baldwin wanted whites to wrestle with what it says about them when they are willing to label and treat others as "niggers." If Baldwin's reasoning is sound, we can also ask what it says about African Americans who take up the 'N' word to use against other people of color in dehumanizing ways.

Baldwin's attempt to shame whites out of using the word against blacks might have worked to effectively kill it, for both cultures, that is, if not for the soon-approaching Black Power Movement which immediately resurrected it. *Take This Hammer* aired in 1964. But around this same time the Black Power Movement was getting under way. As pointed out in the previous chapter, the young movement aimed to breathe new life into the 'N' word; not by shaming whites as Baldwin attempted, but by using it in two distinct ways: the first was to shame blacks out of acting like the scared niggers of the past who would not dare to fight in the revolution, and the second was to give pride to strong blacks by redefining what it meant to be a "nigger," i.e. no longer scared and defeated but dangerous and, if organized, destined to be victorious. The 'N' word could show up in both of these ways in the same sentence and only those who were a part of the culture would be able to differentiate between the two uses. This is the way culture works.

Blaxploitation and the Bad Nigger

The 1970s saw the birth of a new genre of film which, at first, held much promise for members of the Black

Power Movement's attempt to positively redefine the 'N' word. In fact, it can be well argued that the Black Power Movement was responsible for this new genre's initial success. Blaxploitation films are most often remembered for their caricatures of black life; their stereotypical depictions of African Americans as pimps and prostitutes. But that is not how it began.

Most credit the 1971 film *Sweet Sweetback's Badasssss Song* with the birth of the genre. This independent movie told the story of a young, African American man who dared to stand up to the injustice being meted out by white police officers in his neighborhood. Sweetback begins his journey just as unconscious of his significance in the world as many other young blacks. But, progressively, he comes to understand his role and the potential of his entire community to come together to revolutionize the system of oppression under which they live.

The film has been both highly criticized and highly acclaimed. It was one of the first, if not the first, major film to be written, produced, and star an African American (all three functions being performed by the same individual). It also featured a soundtrack with distinct urban flare thanks to the sounds of a little known group (at that time) by the name of Earth, Wind & Fire. But most significantly for history, the film was the first to depict the revolutionary zeal of the Black Power Movement. And yet, it was not the movie that made the movement popular. Rather, it was the other way around.

Just weeks after the movie's release, Black Panther Party co-founder Huey Newton wrote a full analysis of the film. In fact, he dedicated an entire issue of the party's newspaper to the movie. Newton praised the way Sweetback's character went from a state of social unconsciousness to consciousness and felt that the film was able to show black people a way to move forward. This was especially valuable for him during that time because the Black Panther Party's mission was to help black America transition from the era of non-violence to a new day of militancy. Newton was so moved by the portrayal and the messages contained therein, that he made the film mandatory viewing for every person in every chapter of the Black Panther Party all across the United States.[8] Thanks in no small part to this ringing endorsement from the party's leader, the film went on to gross millions of dollars at the box office. And this is where the problems began for the genre. What happens in a commercial-based society when something proves to be profitable? In the name of capitalism and healthy competition, others will rush in to saturate and then oversaturate the market with similar products as they look to cash in on the latest trend.

This led to a barrage of movies throughout the 70s which were produced by black artists and for black audiences. One notable film that grew into a series was that which told of *The Legend of Nigger Charlie*. The 'N' word in the title is a dead give-away that this was a period piece; a sub-genre within the broader category. All Blaxploitation films were not based in the inner-city of the 1970s. Quite a few were based in the antebellum or Reconstruction era South while others were westerns. The *Nigger Charlie* series touches both of these as a pair of escaped slaves head west and eventually (in the third film *Boss Nigger*) become sheriff and deputy of a western town.

But why was the 'N' word in the title acceptable? Was it simply because the film depicted the time period when slavery existed in America? This is doubtful. It must be remembered that these films were not marketed to whites but to blacks who were interested in seeing a different type of "nigger" on screen than what had been previously allowed. The 'N' word in the title is a commentary on the militant spirit of the late 1960s and early 70s. This story of African Americans who were courageous enough to steal away from the system of oppression that was slavery fit right in with the attitude of the Black Power Movement. In fact, by the time the two ex-slaves are seen again in the film *Boss Nigger*, they have created new laws in the town which they police; laws which enable them to jail whites for calling them "nigger" in public. Whites could not say it, but the viewing black audience understood the revisionist, militant message in the film's title – *Nigger Charlie* was the celebration of a new and different type of nigger than what history had heretofore seen.

There were other films during these years, most of which featured the trademark elements of the genre: funk and soul music soundtracks, a focus on black life with a majority black cast, and some element of militancy in one or two righteous characters as an homage to the Black Power spirit of the age. But increasingly, these films featured ignoble images of African Americans as the nation's uneducated, undignified and criminal element – Niggers! Not the bold, educated and dedicated souls of whom the Black Power Movement's leaders would approve. Not the new, dangerous niggers that Stokely Carmichael threatened whites with, but instead, the kind that white America did not need a movie screen to imagine. In fact, over time, all that Blaxploitation served to accomplish was to confirm and perpetuate the stereotype that had existed already for too many years.

James Baldwin tried to pin the 'N' word onto whites. The Black Power movement tried to re-invent the word with what they knew to be true about young, militant blacks. But it soon became evident that the stigma and the stereotype was too strong to be switched off simply by semantics. It remained too difficult to see how the old version of the nigger could ever be supplanted by a new nigger of any kind. Already, by the end of 1972, the NAACP and other civil rights groups had come together to form a Coalition Against Blacksploitation. The founder of the coalition, Junius Griffin commented, "We will not tolerate the continued warping of our children's minds with the filth, violence, and cultural lies that are all-pervasive in current productions of so-called black movies."[9]

These "black movies" did two important things, one positive and the other, very questionable, morally speaking. First, they opened the door for blacks in the film industry like never before. The roles were no longer just cooks and butlers or servants of some kind. Instead, blacks were now getting lead roles and doing the writing and scoring of many films. This was huge historically. Second, even though the Blaxploitation films of the 1970s had gotten away from the consciousness that Huey Newton praised Sweet Sweetback for achieving, there was still something revolutionary happening on the screen – a kind of poetic [in]justice which was lost on the Coalition Against Blacksploitation. Drug-dealers and pimps had become the heroes of Black-Hollywood, alluding police and enjoying the fruit of their illegal labor. Since many young, inner-city blacks had come to see the police as their primary or, at least, most tangible enemy, these romanticized images of blacks living above the law became celebrated folklore. But just why had law enforcement officers come to be viewed in such a negative way? The answer to this question is the hinge upon which it all swings.

Bad Meaning Bad

Many historians, sociologists and criminologists have made the connection between the end of segregation and the United States' declaration of the "War on Crime" with its "Get Tough" slogans and policies. For instance, in her book *The New Jim Crow*, Michelle Alexander details the way in which America's overt system of controlling the black population via segregation was converted to a covert system of control using the code-words "criminals," "drugs" and "law and order" to focus police activity on African American men. This tactic was used to gain mass acceptance for the over-policing of black communities. All of this was the political response to the Civil Rights protest of the late 1950s and 60s. During that time, southern politicians could be heard complaining and campaigning on promises of returning American cities to a state of "Law and Order." But who were the law-breakers that America needed to be protected from? It was the Negro. Not all Negroes. But the ones who dared to sit at "whites only" lunch counters, the ones who refused to ride in the back of the bus and who, against police orders, marched through the streets in non-violent protest against unjust local laws that were in violation of federal laws (and even God's laws). It was the historic "bad nigger" who was causing all the problems.

From 1969 to 1974, Richard Nixon was president of the United States. According to H. R. Haldeman, Nixon's chief of staff before the Watergate scandal, the President saw that "the whole problem is really the blacks," and that "the key is to devise a system that recognizes this while not appearing to."[10] This desire to paint blacks as the problem "while not appearing to" birthed the "Get Tough" on crime movement which called for swifter action against and stiffer penalties for those suspected and convicted of crimes, even non-violent ones. This became a major component of the conservative, political agenda and has continued through the Reagan and Bush years. Surprisingly, these policies have only strengthened under the administrations of Bill Clinton and Barack Obama.[11] Only recently, in 2015, did lawmakers begin to take seriously the problem of mass incarceration and the over-policing of African American communities.

Even Republican politicians and presidential hopefuls rallied behind the cause of undoing the damage wrought by the policies put in place by Nixon and his successors. In the second Republican presidential debate of 2015, when candidates were asked about legalizing marijuana, Senator Rand Paul denounced the hypocrisy that exists in a nation where many whites don't get arrested for possessing or using marijuana while "the people going to jail for it is poor people and often, African Americans and Hispanics." He called for more rehabilitation and less incarceration and noted that "the war on drugs has had a racial outcome" that "has damaged the inner-cities."

This change in tone is welcomed today. However, in the 1970s, blacks living under the long arm and heavy hand of local law enforcement and a prejudiced political system, found beating the system, nearly impossible. There was, therefore, a degree of catharsis involved in seeing the gangsters and hustlers of Blaxploitation fame get away with their dirty deeds. If the righteous version of the "bad nigger," who marched in the streets and fought for equality was seen by whites as a criminal deserving of jail-time; then society would now have to deal with the unrighteous version of the "bad nigger" getting away with murder and making a fortune on the black market (pun intended). This reflects what African American journalist James T. Fortune observed in 1884 concerning the double-edged potential of his newly freed kinsmen:

> When the government freed the slaves and gave the vote, it added four million men . . . to the laboring masses. . . . It also added four millions of souls to what have been termed "the dangerous classes"—meaning, the vast army of men and women who threaten to take by force from society that which society prevents them from making honestly.[12]

The depiction of black pushers and pimps on the screen during the 1970s may have moved away from the consciousness of the Black Power movement; but the anti-establishment message was being communicated nonetheless. Many minorities in the inner-city lived with an "us versus them" mentality towards the system of oppression represented by law enforcement officials. And both versions of the "bad nigger" were out to prove just how dangerous the lower classes could be when made to feel trapped. Under these circumstances it is, perhaps, understandable that many young blacks celebrated Blaxploitation films despite their questionable moral implications.

While it is true that some blacks went outside the boarders of the law during the 1970s in order to make their fortune through criminal enterprise, glorifying that lifestyle through the medium of film surely sent a confusing message, especially to the inner-city youth who gave birth to Hip Hop culture within that same decade. As we will see in the next chapter, many Hip Hop pioneers were young, impressionable children during that time. And while some chose to emulate the more conscious and organized version of the "bad nigger," many others would use their eventual rap careers to celebrate and relive the tales of the unrighteous hood-heroes of Blaxploitation fame.

Suffice to say that as the 1970s came to a close, black America, and America as a whole for that matter, was dealing with two different types of "bad niggers": those who were "bad" in the eyes of whites because they were willing to break unjust laws in order to fight for justice, and those who were "bad" even in the eyes of many blacks because they were willing to violate just laws in order to escape poverty and live the American dream.

Herein lies the problem with embracing the concept of the "bad nigger" after the advent of Blaxploitation. There is the potential of confusing what it means to be "bad" with what it means to be "good." To call self-destructive and community crippling behavior "good" is as illogical as racism itself. A person may use the lack of jobs in a community to justify pimping, prostitution and pushing drugs – activities which draw police into a community to enforce the law. This same person might then complain about the excessive and oppressive presence of police in the neighborhood while, at the same time, celebrating the success of pimps, prostitutes and pushers who have gotten over on the system. "That's a *baaad* nigga, right there," someone might say of the neighborhood hustler. Like Run DMC, they don't mean "bad meaning bad but bad meaning good." In this way, one attempts to pin the same badge of honor onto the pimp or pusher as one might to the 19th century runaway slave or the 20th century leaders of the Black Power Movement. The impression given is that it does not matter; for a black man in America, being *baaad* is always good. This mindset has reverberated down through the years and has implications for the African American high schooler who takes pride in being bad, disrupting the classroom in his school dominated by white teachers and administration.

But this was not always the way. Originally, when Stokely Carmichael voiced the desire for Black Power, he meant that black people should band together and make their political presence felt in order to change unjust laws in their community. But, what the criminality of the Blaxploitation era showcased was not a standing together, but a looking out for oneself at the expense of the community. This kind of "bad" had never been seen as good before that time. But, since then, whenever "bad" meets "nigger" almost anything is justifiable because of the moral compromise that seems to come along with the territory.

No Laughing Matter

Hannibal Burress was not alone in the summer of 2015 when he attempted humor concerning the "colored people" portion of the N.A.A.C.P. acronym. Just one month after his *Why* promo aired, another comedian targeted the civil rights group. In episode five of the ninth season of NBC's *Last Comic Standing*, comedian Harrison Greenbaum made the observation that "It's not that advanced" for the N.A.A.C.P. to still be using the term "colored people." But he claimed to understand why they could not update the terminology to "African Americans." If they were to do this "then their group name would just be Nah" (N.A.A.A.A.). The crowd gave a cautious laugh. But one of the show's three judges, veteran comedian Norm McDonald, a Caucasian man no less, sternly critiqued Greenbaum with a warm smile. "There is a reason that the organization is called the N.A.A.C.P.; maybe you can research it, find out what it is and then not do the joke anymore," Norm advised.

It remains necessary to affirm the humanity of colored individuals and by constantly referring to them as "people" this aim is accomplished. But some argue that the continued use of the 'N' word achieves the same goal by using irony to point out how blacks are viewed and treated in America. No one uses irony better than comedians. These individuals are known for making keen observations about common, yet seldom articulated, social realities. They find and fixate on contradictions and absurdities. And so it is no surprise that many black comics have made the 'N' word a staple of their stage performance. This was truer for one comedian than, probably any other in the past forty years; the legendary Richard Pryor. Pryor built his career on the 'N' word, forcing the nation to become acquainted with the "niggers" it had created. He made fierce social commentary and invited crowds to laugh through the pain of the black experience in America. But it wasn't until he left the country's shore that he realized the impact of his favorite word.

James Baldwin believed that the "nigger" was a specifically American problem that did not exist in any other country in the world. One could challenge this view considering the way in which Aborigines in Australia, for instance, or blacks in South Africa during apartheid have been treated by whites. But, interestingly, Richard Pryor seems to have come to a similar conclusion as Baldwin during a trip to Africa. There, he had a change of heart concerning the 'N' word which came, not by evolution but, through an epiphany.

In 1968, several years before his epiphany, Richard Pryor was joking about the imagined exploits of a black super hero. Right away, one notices a certain "ghetto-esque" quality to this fictional character. A white hero is a Superman. But since niggers are subhuman, when someone who is black becomes super, he simply graduates to finally being a man. The name of

Pryor's hero, therefore, is not Superman, but Super-Nigger. Being simply and finally a normal man, Super-Nigger is plagued by things perceived as common to the average person, e.g. having a dead-end, low-paying job and an illegal drug habit. But as he springs into action, he does have a few powers which make him heroic to blacks in the late 1960s. Yes he can fly, but that is not as important as his ability to confront whites about calling him "Nigger" even though the 'N' word is a part of his moniker. Only blacks can call on him by name.

A few years later, in 1974, Pryor performed his famed stand-up routine *That Nigger's Crazy* in which he contrasts the lifestyles of "white people" and "niggas" almost the entire time. The sheer number of times and ways in which he uses the 'N' word during his set shows its comfortable place in black life during the mid-70s. But by 1982, the comedian had had a powerful experience which changed his thoughts on the matter. While in Africa, Pryor recalls that one day as he looked around, he could sense a voice probing him with the thoughtful question, "What do you see?" His response – "I see all colors of people doing everything." The voice then asked him a profound question, "Do you see any niggers?" "No," Pryor answered. "Do you know why?" the voice asked before enlightening him with the answer, "because there aren't any." And with that, a light flashed in his soul, illuminating his understanding.

It was not that there were no black people within his view, for all he saw was gradations of black and brown skin everywhere his eyes fell. Only, there were no niggers. "Oh my God!" Pryor exclaimed in that moment, "I've been wrong . . . I ain't never gonna call another black man 'nigger.'"

Was Richard joking? The audience at the Sunset Strip was unsure, at first. Should they laugh? But then, some began to get the impression that not only should they not laugh; but perhaps they should applaud. This was a monumental moment for the man who had built his career offering commentary on the life of the nigger; the man who could not go more than thirty seconds on stage without saying the word. Pryor had been in Africa three weeks at the time of his epiphany and claims that he hadn't said or even thought the word the entire time he was there. For some reason, (and this was James Baldwin's point) "nigger" seemed to only fit in the American context.

It has been said that it takes twenty-one days to break a habit. What would the outcome be if more African Americans were to take a three week hiatus from using the 'N' word and spend that time investing in changing the way they see themselves and other black and brown people? Almost twenty years after *Take This Hammer* aired, Richard Pryor had come to the same conclusion as James Baldwin. "We never was no niggers," Pryor informed his crowd. "That's a word that has been used to describe our own wretchedness and we perpetuate it now cuz that word is dead now. We're men and women." For him, being a nigger meant accepting the notion that blacks are sub-human. And in order to live as men and women that word had to die, not simply have its meaning changed.

Perhaps this explains the virtual absence of the 'N' word in the stand-up comedy work of the next African American comic to take the stage and country by storm. Eddie Murphy grew up idolizing Richard Pryor. He recalls how he used to sneak down to the basement to listen to Pryor's raunchy *That Nigger's Crazy* album over and over again. Murphy knew that he wanted to be just like this man. But the other comedian he had grown up revering was Bill Cosby, who had a completely different comedic style. During the 1987 filming of his *Raw* show, Eddie Murphy recounted how he received conflicting advice from these two, elder, satirical statesmen. Bill Cosby, of all people, had called Eddie Murphy to chastise him for his dirty jokes and foul language on stage. It was, according to Cosby, Murphy's responsibility to present a better role-model for black youth. Murphy then called Richard Pryor for advice, who encouraged him to continue to do his jokes in his own way as long as people were laughing and Murphy was making money. Which of his two childhood heroes would Eddie Murphy take his marching orders from? It was of course, Pryor's advice that won out.

Murphy continued to be as brash and abrasive as he saw fit. He would not tone it down and play nice as Bill Cosby commanded. And yet, in Murphy's first nationally televised stand-up sensation *Delirious* (just one year after Richard Pryor's 1982 "I'm never gonna call another black man nigger" declaration), Eddie only used the 'N' word five times: once while speaking as the character of his own drunken father, and the other four times while commenting about the way whites see and refer to black people. Four years later, his second nationally televised routine *Raw* aired. This time, the comedian used the 'N' word a total of twelve times, once while speaking through the character of "vindictive black women," once, jokingly, to refer to black men in the crowd who were ignorant of a point he was making, and ten times while making statements about racism and stereotypes. Of those ten, eight were spoken as white characters created by Murphy.

Five times in *Delirious* and twelve times in *Raw* might seem like a lot of 'N' words to be throwing around, but not for a comedian who grew up studying Richard Pryor. Not for the comedian who had received Pryor's blessing to defy Bill Cosby by being as foul-mouthed as he deemed fit. Murphy said every raunchy thing Pryor had said and more! But when he wanted to refer to black men, he did not use the word his mentor had denounced on the Sunset Strip in 1982. Instead, Murphy referred to black men over and over again in both films as "brothers."

Pryor had learned (and taught) that carrying the 'N' word also meant carrying the negative idea behind it. And that even while he was trying to help Americans cope with the word's black history, the word was creating new negative history each time it was used to name or shame his people. It is not that he was not man enough to defeat it, but precisely because he was a man, and not a nigger, he would no longer use it. This influenced those who followed in his steps.

Was this it? The end? The death of the 'N' word? Had these two funnymen, these hilarious truth-tellers, killed the nasty name? Had Frodo completed his mission and delivered his evil parcel into the fires of Mount Mordor? Was this, at least, the beginning of a trend that could catch on where the word would eventually die and disappear from the African American vocabulary? History would not give the necessary time for this to happen. For just one year after Eddie Murphy's *Raw* aired, the 'N' word was resurrected with a strength that it never before possessed – the strength of street knowledge.

3

Navigating the Strength of Street Knowledge

"You are now about to witness the strength of street knowledge." These are the ominous words heard at the very beginning of a 1988 rap album which forever changed urban, youth culture; and, for that matter, American culture as a whole. The album was N.W.A.'s *Straight Outta Compton*. For those unaware, N.W.A. stood for Niggaz Wit Attitude. Compton is a city in the state of California which underwent the typical inner-city experience of white flight and urban blight in the 1970s. Integral to this discussion, it must be asked, in what way did N.W.A. change America?

Was it just that the group introduced Gangster Rap on a commercially successful level? "Gangster Rap" is that style of rap music which originally began to glamorize violence and crime as the way of life for young, black males in the inner-cities of America. There is no doubt that this is one important way in which N.W.A. effected change, for they did not simply present themselves as a musical group. In the very first line of the first song on their first album, the group is called a "gang" by one of its most vocal members, Ice Cube. If this was more than simply a figure of speech, then the title "Gangster Rap" is aptly applied. And it can be well argued that they were the first Gangster Rap group, the ones who put this particular brand of rap music on the map.

Although the West Coast is often thought of as the birth-place of Gangster Rap, this view can be challenged. For starters, N.W.A. is not where this category of rap began. Rapper-turned-actor Ice T (not to be confused with Ice Cube) is often credited as the "Original Gangster" rapper. Born Tracie Marrow, Ice T may have earned his stripes (and fame) on the West Coast, but his place of origin was on the East Coast in New Jersey, not far from Hip Hop's birthplace of New York. However, the argument that 'Gangster Rap is not an entirely West Coast creation' does not rest squarely on Ice T's East Coast roots. It also rests on the fact that Ice T openly admits to having received the inspiration for his streetwise songs from the man he believes officially to be the first Gangster Rapper: the Philadelphia born and bred Hip Hop legend, Schooly D. In 1985, Schooly D released the record "P.S.K. What Does it Mean?" to shout out his neighborhood gang. The album was soaked in scenes of urban realism that was rarely heard in early 1980s rap. However, the trend was not immediately followed by other urban artists. Thus, it was not until the commercial success of N.W.A. that Gangster Rap became a staple in the American music diet.

Still, this is not the only way in which N.W.A. changed American culture. It will be demonstrated that it was the success of this group's music that reintroduced the 'N' word into the vernacular of popular black art. And it will be further shown that prior to the release of the *Straight Outta Compton* album, the notorious name, Nigger, was dying a slow death on the world's stage.

Three Objections

There are three main objections to the above claim that must be answered. First is the objection that "Even if the 'N' word was disappearing from African American public life, it does not mean that blacks were not using it in private." Second, the objection is raised that "Even if N.W.A. did reintroduce the word into African American art, it does not mean that they meant to resurrect the negative aspects of it. They may have only meant to use it in a rhetorical sense." Third, and lastly, there is the demand for proof to back up the above claim. Taking it for granted that Hip Hop culture, represented by rap music, is recognized as the voice of the generation which followed the Civil Rights and the Black Power movements, the questions is, "Would a survey of Hip Hop history support the idea that rappers were uninterested in "niggas" before the 1988 release of *Straight Outta Compton*, but became obsessed with the word after the album's release?" Each of these objections will be dealt with in turn.

Objection #1

"Even if the 'N' word was being removed from African American public life, it does not mean that blacks were not using it in private." This objection has some weight. Before the term "Gangster Rap" was coined, N.W.A. and others labeled their brand of music "Reality Rap." And so, when they spoke of "niggas," perhaps they were simply reflecting the reality of how the average black person spoke 'off camera.' In that case, if N.W.A. were the ones who reintroduced the 'N' word into the public sphere, this could mean that other rappers before them were not representing reality. But there is another possibility. It could be that, before this time, rappers simply chose to deal with reality differently. Consider the old adage, "At first art will imitate life, but soon after, life will begin to imitate art." Knowing this, an artist can intentionally choose to put forth an image in his art which is not yet true in real life or in his culture but instead, gives others within the culture something to shoot for and imitate.

So even though the 'N' word might have been in the mouth of the average person, if it was on its way out of black art before 1988, it could be that artists were projecting the image they wanted to see imitated at the street level. One could ask, 'which artistic approach is more effective: reflecting reality or projecting what the reality could, or maybe, should be?' Reason would suggest that reflecting and projecting are equally valuable at different times and on different occasions. Sometimes it may be necessary to accurately, artistically depict the real life situation that a particular people-group is facing. This is good because it gives a sense of where a culture or society is in its development; of how far people have come and how far they have yet to go. At other times it will be necessary to cast a vision, not of where people are but of where they could get to and how they can arrive at their desired destination. That African American artists, and particularly rappers, tried at all costs to avoid the 'N' word prior to 1988 may not have been a reflection of how all blacks were living. But it might have been a projection of how blacks wanted to live – free of the stigma of being "niggas."

Consider also the "eight pillars of culture" introduced in the forward to this book. The cultural questions associated with *art* are: what ideas, events and emotions are worth reproducing; and how skillfully or uniquely can this be done? Recall, also, that it is the answers to the *values* questions which strengthen or weaken the other pillars. Therefore, the exclusion of the 'N' word prior to 1988 could have been a silent social commentary from rappers that there was nothing valuable, nothing worth reproducing as it pertains to the word "nigger."

Objection #2

"Even if N.W.A. did reintroduce the word into African American art, it does not mean that they meant to resurrect its negative implications. They may have only meant it in a rhetorical sense." This objection is based on the semantic range of the word and might hold up in some cases, though not in all. Upon surveying the data, one finds that there were both seemingly positive and negative uses of "nigga" in the group's vernacular. It will be shown, however, that even the seemingly positive uses are better categorized as "not-*as*-negative but still negative" uses. In fact, there appears to be three main ways in which the 'N' word is used in Hip Hop today which are a direct result of its reintroduction in 1988: there is the Expendable Nigga, the Dependable Nigga, and the Exceptional Nigga.

The Expendable Nigga – four uses

The "Expendable Nigga" is the most common, and also the most complex category. It is, for that very reason, the largest of the three. There are four ways in which the word "nigga" is used to refer to someone as "expendable." This may sound confusing at first but think of the movie Antwone Fisher. In one scene the main character recalls how his foster mother used to address him and his two foster brothers. They were, all, each referred to as "Nigga" but the boys came to know which brother she was referring to by the way she uttered the word. Similarly and sadly, many African Americans grow up knowing how to decipher between these four uses of the "expendable nigga" without having to exercise much thought at all.

1. The first of the four is inherited from the history of its usage upon white lips. An expendable nigga is one whose life can be taken without giving it a second thought because at the end of the day, what is taken is not the life of a person with value but the life of something sub-human. At the street level, an expendable nigga is anyone who stands in the way of the resources I am seeking: be it, food, financial gain, a female, or fame. If I can obtain my perceived needs at the expense of this person's life or wellbeing, then so be it. He or she is an expendable nigga. More bluntly, it is precisely because the individual standing in my way is black or brown, aka a nigga, that his or her life is expendable. (Interestingly, unlike when the word was used by whites, within the domain of Hip Hop, "nigga" is almost exclusively used for males. There is another term reserved for expendable females which will be explored in chapter eight)

   e.g. On the *Doggystyle* album, rapper Snoop Dogg depicts a scenario where he is confronted by another male whose girlfriend finds Snoop so irresistible that she instantly leaves her boyfriend to be with the rapper. When confronted, Snoop explains the situation to his rival thusly: "You know what it is nigga, your b*tch chose me." Seconds later the incident comes to a bloody end with Snoop shooting the individual dead. In Snoop's defense, he did give his rival in this scenario the option to handle the situation like gentleman or like "gangsters." But the fact remains, the life of his rival was expendable, worthless compared to what Snoop stood to gain.

2. The expendable nigga is also used in an ironic sense. It is as if to say to America, to the collective conscience of the country, "Hey! I'm a black man who is supposedly free, and no longer a slave. Constitutionally, I have the same rights as anyone else. I can go to school where I want. Live where I want. Vote. Marry outside of my race. I can go to the same places of business as my white friends. I can make music and art that entertains the nation. I can compete on the world stage athletically. I can make more money than my white teachers back in grade-school could ever dream of. But it's ironic that somehow, even after all that, in this racist system we live under, I am still treated as if my life is just as expendable as my forefathers' centuries ago. I am still just a nigga." Often times, rappers use the phrase this way to refer to themselves in the third

person. But it is only as they see themselves through America's eyes. Not that they actually see themselves as expendable, but rather, that they are made to feel that way. It is always a cry for pity or mercy when used this way.

e.g. A person may be heard saying, "Can a nigga get a break?"

e.g. Referring to the way the cops treat him, in the song "F*ck the Police" Ice Cube raps, "I don't know if they fags or what/ search a nigga down and grabbin' his nuts."

3. The expendable nigga is also used via its shaming power. This occurs when the one speaking does not mean to convey that the life of a particular individual is expendable, but rather, that the person being called a "nigga" is acting in a way that warrants him or her being temporarily disregarded. Not that the person's life should be totally discounted; but their presence or their position on a certain subject; or at the very least, the person's most recent remark in the conversation is expendable.

e.g. When Phife Dawg from the rap-group A Tribe Called Quest lyrically confronts those who would bootleg his music on the song "Show Business" he raps "Please nigga, I've worked too hard for this."

e.g. On the song "Vapors" when Biz Markie tells the story of one of his friends trying to flirt with a woman who is "out of his league," the woman's response to his friend's rap is, "Nigga please, you work for UPS."

4. The final way in which the term "nigga" is used to refer to someone as expendable is when it is done in jest, i.e. jokingly. When the word is used this way it is clear that the one speaking does not actually see the life of the one he is referring to as expendable. If it is possible for this poisonous word to be emptied of its venom, it is only the rapport between the two individuals that takes the sting out of it and allows them to joke this way. When a word that would normally cause friction is used sarcastically between two friends, it is viewed as proof that two individuals are closer than what their antagonistic rhetoric may suggest. Clearly, if any harm or ill-will was intended, the parties involved would not be able to use such a volatile word as "nigga" without the situation escalating into full-fledged violence.

e.g. In the song "Jingling Baby" rapper L.L. Cool J ends his final verse by talking down to other rappers who are unable to compete with him. He raps, "I'ma deliver and give a speech with vigor/ drink some O.E. and start waxing niggas." At first, this sounds like a case of the

"Expendable nigga" #1 discussed above. However, it is not a serious matter of life and death. No one is really being called "expendable" here. This is clearly seen when, on the remix, L.L. changes the last line to "Pass the wine-cooler you big, black nigga" while he laughs light-heartedly.

These four uses are grouped together because, no matter which of them is being employed at any given time, those who are being referred to are still being conditioned to accept some negative application of the term "nigga" as a fitting designation for oneself. At the subconscious level, the sentiment that "I am" or "something about me is expendable" is further adopted and owned. On top of this, in order to be able to call someone a "nigga" in any one of these four ways, the speaker has to assume a dominant position and that he or she has the right to name another person in this way.

The Dependable Nigga

The dependable nigga is much less complex and therefore requires little explanation. It is almost like the fourth usage of the "expendable nigga" because of the relational element involved. But here, there is not even the hint of a joke that the referent is seen as expendable. In fact, quite the opposite. The dependable nigga is emphatically used to convey the idea that even though the referent might be expendable to others, he or she is not expendable to the speaker. The one speaking depends on the one being called "my nigga" and cannot do without the service or companionship that he or she provides. This is referred to as the "term of endearment."

e.g. Any modern rap song could be cited here, but one of the earliest examples of rappers giving shout-outs to "My nigga so&so" at the end of a song is the artist Redman on the record "Down Wit Us" where he proclaims, "My nigga Erick Sermon is down wit us." Before then, it was more customary for rappers to shout out "my man", "my brother" or "my homeboy so&so."

Note: More recently, it has become common for urban-dwellers and those influenced by Hip Hop culture to use the term "my nigga" to address those who are on the verge of becoming expendable. In tense situations "What's up my nigga?" is a question that functions rather rhetorically to alert the one being addressed that he has mere seconds to endear himself to the speaker before things reach the critical point of no return and become violent. The rhetorical nature of the question rests on the fact that there is often too much pride involved for the one being addressed as "my nigga" to say or do anything to endear himself to the speaker in the heat of the moment, e.g. apologize, explain himself or do anything to de-escalate the situation. As will be shown in chapter six, the fact that "my nigga" can be so easily converted to an "expendable nigga" shows the danger of embracing the word as a proper designation, even as a term of endearment.

The Exceptional Nigga

The exceptional nigga is rare, rarely mentioned in music and, perhaps rarely seen in the streets. Yet, almost everyone who self-identifies as a "nigga" believes he is an exceptional nigga and not the common expendable one. But to achieve this level of individualization one must possess or be able to do something that other "niggas" do not or cannot. Often, the one thing the exceptional nigga needs to possess is an undying commitment to the rules of the "game" and the code of the streets, i.e. hustling and being a bad nigga. Many adjectives are put in front of the 'N' word in order to signify the exceptional nature of the one being labeled a nigga. And often the claim is made in the first person. For instance one might be heard announcing "I'm a *real* nigga," "I'm a *true* nigga," "I'm a *street* nigga," "I'm a *gangsta* nigga," "I'm a *thorough* nigga."

e.g. In Busta Rhymes' song "I'll Hurt You" the rapper covers several uses of the 'N' word in three bars of rhymed speech. Right after he contrasts his own exceptional qualities with the expendable nature of his listeners, Busta remarks how he progressed from being an ironic-expendable nigga in his early days. He raps:

> You know that I'm the *only nigga* that could ever come and spitefully turn the place into a mother-f*ckin' zoo/ then I come and I spit crazy sh*t and make niggas do exactly what I want'em to/ from my point of view instead of trying to step up you're still trying to play catch up and keep up with the way a nigga grew

e.g. In the song "Still Fly" by Big Tymers, rapper Baby details the way he customizes his car with after-market upgrades and then proclaims, "When it comes to these cars I am *that* nigga."

Objection #3

Finally, the claim that *Straight Outta Compton* reintroduced the 'N' word into popular black art at a time when it was dying out is met, not with an objection as much as a demand for proof. It needs to be substantiated before it can be taken seriously.

It is all but undeniable that rap music stood as the most visible and vocal artistic expression of African American, urban culture in the 1980s (as well as in the following decades). Taking this for granted, the following chart surveys fifty-five of the most influential rap albums spanning the ten year period from 1985 to 1994; the decade which covers what Hip Hop aficionados refer to as the "Golden Era of Hip Hop." The albums are listed in chronological order according to their respective release dates. For each album, the number of times the 'N' word is used is counted and each usage is categorized as either a reference to an "Expendable Nigga," a "Dependable Nigga," or an "Exceptional Nigga." Not counted are the number of times the word is used rhetorically; for instance when Ice T says, "A lot of people get mad cuz I use the word 'nigga.'" But rather, what is counted is each time a person is referred to as a nigga/er. Following the chart, in the next two chapters, will be a discussion of what conclusions can be drawn from this data.

(Mark the location of this chart as it will be referred to but not reproduced in subsequent chapters)

"Nigga" in the Golden Era of Hip Hop

Year	Artist	Album	Expend-able Nigga	Depend-able Nigga	Except-ional Nigga	Total 'N' words	Region
1985	Run DMC	King of Rock	0	0	0	0	East Coast
1985	LL Cool J	My Radio	0	0	0	0	East Coast
1985	Schooly D	Schooly D	15	0	0	15	East Coast
1986	Run DMC	Raising Hell	0	0	0	0	East Coast
1986	2 Live Crew	We Are the 2 Live Crew	0	0	0	0	The South
1987	Public Enemy	Yo! Bum Rush the Show	0	0	0	0	East Coast
1987	KRS One	Criminal Minded	0	0	0	0	East Coast
1987	LL Cool J	Bigger and Deffer	0	0	0	0	East Coast
1987	Too $hort	Born to Mack	3	0	0	3	West Coast
1987	Ice T	Rhyme Pays	1	0	0	1	West Coast
1987	Eric B. & Rakim	Paid in Full	0	0	0	0	East Coast
1988	Geto Boys	Making Trouble	0	0	0	0	The South
1988	KRS One	By All Means Necessary	0	0	0	0	East Coast

Year	Artist	Album	Expend-able Nigga	Depend-able Nigga	Except-ional Nigga	Total 'N' words	Region
1988	Big Daddy Kane	Long Live the Kane	0	0	0	0	East Coast
1988	EPMD	Strictly Business	1	0	0	1	East Coast
1988	Public Enemy	It Takes a Nation of Millions to Hold Us Back	1 ½	0	0	1 1/2**	East Coast
1988	Eric B. & Rakim	Follow the Leader	0	0	0	0	East Coast
1988	N.W.A.	Straight Outta Compton	28	0	16	44	West Coast
1988	2 Live Crew	Move Somethin'	63	5	1	69	The South
1988	Ice T	Power	4	0	2	6	West Coast
1988	Slick Rick	The Great Adventures of Slick Rick	0	0	0	0***	East Coast
1988	Jungle Brothers	Straight Out the Jungle	0	0	0	0	East Coast
1989	Too $hort	Life is Too Short	3	0	1	4	West Coast
1989	Geto Boys	Grip It! On A Another Level	28	0	15	43	The South
1989	D.O.C.	No One Can Do It Better	3	0	2	5*	West Coast
1989	Kool G Rap & DJ Polo	Road to the Riches	0	0	0	0	East Coast
1989	Naughty by Nature	Independ-ent Leaders	0	0	0	0	East Coast
1989	EPMD	Unfinished Business	0	0	0	0	East Coast

Year	Artist	Album	Expend-able Nigga	Depend-able Nigga	Except-ional Nigga	Total 'N' words	Region
1989	Big Daddy Kane	It's a Big Daddy Thing	0	0	0	0	East Coast
1990	King Sun	Righteous but Ruthless	22	0	0	22*	East Coast
1990	Above the Law	Living Like Hustlers	3	0	5	8*	West Coast
1990	A Tribe Called Quest	People's Instinctive Travels and Paths of Rhythm	0	0	0	0	East Coast
1990	Public Enemy	Fear of A Black Planet	5	0	2	7	East Coast
1990	Ice Cube	Amerikkka's Most Wanted	34	0	18	52	West Coast
1990	KRS One	Edutain-ment	8	0	0	8**	East Coast
1990	Paris	The Devil Made Me Do It	2	1	0	3**	West Coast
1990	Brand Nubian	All for One	0	0	0	0	East Coast
1991	Master P	Get Away Clean	28	6	7	41	West Coast
1991	Ice T	Original Gangster	59	8	24	91	West Coast
1991	Naughty By Nature	Naughty By Nature	9	0	2	11	East Coast
1991	A Tribe Called Quest	Low End Theory	1	0	0	1*	East Coast
1991	2Pac	2Pacaly-pse Now	60	0	25	85	West Coast
1992	Gang Starr	Daily Operation	10	0	0	10	East Coast

Year	Artist	Album	Expend-able Nigga	Depend-able Nigga	Except-ional Nigga	Total 'N' words	Region
1992	Redman	What? Thee Album	13	5	2	20	East Coast
1992	Common Sense	Can I Borrow A Dollar	19	1	1	21	Chicago /East Coast
1992	Kool G Rap & DJ Polo	Live and Let Die	145	0	6	151	East Coast
1993	8 Ball & MJG	Coming Out Hard	77	3	13	93	The South
1993	Wu Tang Clan	Enter the Wu Tang: 36 Chambers	92	3	1	96	East Coast
1993	A Tribe Called Quest	Midnight Marauders	70	0	2	72	East Coast
1993	Snoop Dogg	Doggy-style	113	17	5	135	West Coast
1994	Nas	Illmatic	50	2	0	52	East Coast
1994	Outkast	Southern-playalisti-cadalac-muzik	94	8	11	113	The South
1994	UGK	Super Tight	139	16	35	190	The South
1994	Common Sense	Resurrect-ion	33	4	2	39	Chicago /East Coast
1994	The Notorious B.I.G.	Ready to Die	92	8	2	102	East Coast

* 'N' word is used by guest but not by main artist

** N word is used but never in a expendable (#1) sense

*** 'N' word is only used in a skit on the album

The numbers themselves do not tell the full story. It will take some knowledge of Hip Hop history to decipher just what all of this means. To that end, chapters four and five are devoted to a careful analysis of this chart. As the focus of the book shifts very heavily to Hip Hop culture, it would be a mistake to view this as a departure from the African American history of chapters one and two. In fact, something amazing happens when Hip Hop is treated like the history that it is. What follows is not merely a discussion of rap albums, but of culturally significant moments that shaped a generation and changed the trajectory of a would-be movement—a movement that could have, and perhaps, should have followed the Civil Rights and Black Power movements.

In order to gain the full effect, the reader should envision his or herself on the inner-city streets of America during the time of each of these musical releases, and attempt to estimate the impact of each cultural shift as it came, line by line; each struggle to resist the new norm and then, the seemingly inevitable acceptance of the trend. Notice how the negative force that these cultural leaders thought they were overthrowing, ends up overpowering the culture. Lastly, bear in mind that Rap music is not 'just music.' Rather, its representations of manhood and rhythmic mantras have raised untold numbers of fatherless males from the inner-city to the suburbs; from Native American reservations to Aboriginal youth in Australia. Be it verily, virtually or vicariously, what follows is a history that belongs to these groups as well.

Analyzing the Chart

The above survey begins with the calendar year 1985 partly because most regard the late 1980s to the mid-90s as Hip Hop's "Golden Era." The exact beginning of the era differs depending on who is giving the account. Perhaps it is best to let those who were a part of the history guide our understanding. Rapper Ice T once credited the legendary New York group Run DMC with resurrecting, or at least resuscitating rap music when it was on the brink of death in the early 80s. The group's first album was released in 1984 and brought a fresh sound to the genre. The beats were more hardcore and the lyrics more aggressive than that of Hip Hop past. But Run DMC did something else which set them apart.

In the early 80s, rap music was primarily about partying, how good the rapper's Dj was, and how much each rapper thought he was better than other rappers. Upon their entrance, however, Run DMC took a page from Grand Master Flash and Furious Five's 1982 hit song "The Message" which actually talked about social issues and the struggle of inner-city life. Run DMC did talk about traditional rap subjects (sucker MCs and girls) but they also had a strong strand of consciousness woven throughout their music. You will recall from the previous chapter that, in the eyes of the leaders of the Black Power Movement, it was individual and social consciousness (along with organization) that helped to graduate the common street "nigga" to the status of being one of the righteous "bad niggas" that the black community needed.

In 1985, Run DMC followed up their debut album with their second offering, *King of Rock* where they continued their blend of bragging on their talent, battling other would-be competitors and bemoaning anti-social behaviors. In that same year, however, two other albums were released which had historical significance. One was L.L. Cool J's *My Radio* and the other, Schooly D's self-titled freshman album. Together, these three albums represent the choice which every rapper over the following decade would have to make, namely, what kind of rapper am I going to be and what am I going to rap about?

L.L. Cool J's "My Radio" simply carried on the tradition of rapping about one's self, belittling the competition and collecting female followers along the way. Schooly D's album was the origin of Hip Hop celebrating the "bad nigga." This was not the historical "bad nigga" who was "good" in the eyes of black folks who wanted change but "bad" in the eyes of those supporting the racist status quo. Rather, it was the celebration of the "bad nigga" who was bad for no good reason, willing to treat others as expendable in order to look out for oneself. He bragged about carrying and using automatic weapons and threatened to knock out his competition. Rappers had made disparaging remarks about other rappers before then, but for the first time, while listening to Schooly D, listeners were left with the impression that the rapper was not talking figuratively about his foes, but quite literally. He was a *baaad* dude!

Almost two years later, L.L. Cool J was back and he was *Bigger and Deffer*, or so his album titled claimed. "I'm Bad" the first single from the album might have convinced some people to put L.L. in the same category as Schooly D. but it was obvious to many that the two rappers were not the same kind of bad. For starters, L.L.'s opponents were always other rappers and at the end of the day, listeners are left with the impression that his opponents are still alive when he is through with them. Whereas Schooly D, at least in his early career, seemed to be bringing real neighborhood strife to his songs. One of the clear differences was seen in the way the two artists addressed their foes. For L.L., the competition was sucker MCs. But for Schooly D, the opposition was expendable "niggas." L.L. uttered the 'N' word zero times in his first two albums whereas Schooly D had used it fifteen times in his first album alone. (As per the chart, notice that Schooly D is alone in this trend in the mid-80s.)

From across the country, on the West Coast, Ice T praised Run DMC for their contribution to Hip Hop. But he also saw a high value in what Schooly D brought to the table. These two musical acts represented two different types of "bad niggas." Yet, Ice T struggled with the definition of "bad" being offered by L.L. Cool J. In fact, on his 1988 album *Power*, Ice T harshly critiqued

L.L. for having elementary subject matter in his raps. Making fun of L.L.'s "I'm Bad" claim, Ice T challenged him to upgrade his rhymes from talking about himself to talking about something that really matters. In one line he accuses, "You ain't never kicked knowledge one time." "Kicking knowledge" in Hip Hop vernacular simply means educating the culture on issues that will contribute to the mental and social health of the people. Ice T. tells L.L. that he has a "weak mind" which creates "weak rhymes."

The subject matter of East Coast rap (partying and being able to out-rap other rappers at the party) was frustrating for West Coast rappers and for Ice T in particular. In several of his early songs, Ice T admits to the struggle he felt as it pertained to his own artistry. Should he follow the lead of Schooly D and be a Gangster Rapper, depicting the street life he claimed to know so well? Or should he attempt to do what most New York rappers were doing? On the song "Original Gangster," Ice T confessed "When I write about parties, someone always dies" in his songs. That was his environment and on one hand, he felt he had to reflect it. On the other, he respected Run DMC's attempt to project an image for the culture to embrace and grow into. But there was no room in the middle for what L.L. was doing, i.e. art that neither reflected nor projected a cultural image but instead, only presented a certain individual as exceptional.

Being exceptional has always been key to East Coast Hip Hop. And yet, with all the talk of exceptionalism, there was no mention of the exceptional nigga. In fact, there was hardly any mention of niggas at all. As the above survey shows, exceptional niggas were not the subject of rap music until after the culture had become oversaturated with mentions of expendable ones. This progression occurred first on the West Coast. But there are two very interesting and powerful reasons as to why, on the East Coast, this trend was resisted. That is the subject of the remainder of this book.

4

Navigating the Strength of
Street Knowledge (Part 2)

Ice T, and others on the West Coast, not only embraced it but, they sought to imitate Schooly D's overt street lyricism which many have credited as the fountain-head of Gangster Rap. There is a reason for this regional embrace; but there is also a reason why Gangster Rap did not immediately catch on along the East Coast. Both the East and the West had experienced encounters with gang life and the party scene, but the experience occurred in reverse order from one coast to the other, and this made all the difference.

Hip Hop was originally born in the Bronx, NY during a time when feuding street gangs had successfully orchestrated a truce, leaving the borough in a state of relative peace and calm. In this violence-free environment, impromptu block-parties became the breeding grounds for the artistic and technological innovations which came to be known as the four basic elements of Hip Hop culture, i.e. DJ-ing, Break-dancing, Rapping and Graffiti.

Much like *Sweet Sweetback's Badasssss Song*, many early Hip Hop pioneers had a moment of clarity and consciousness as they became aware of the social significance of rap music. They realized that the creativity of these ghetto youths could serve a higher purpose than just entertaining at block parties. Afrika Bambaataa was one such pioneer. Using his influence as a high-ranking member of the Black Spades street gang, Afrika Bambaataa morphed his association into the cultural organization known as the Zulu Nation. This group would go on to spread an organized understanding of Hip Hop culture and life all over the world. Remember that, along with consciousness, organization is one of the marks that a street nigga has become a righteous, bad nigga in the eyes of the leaders of the Black Power Movement.

Another pioneer along those lines was Hip Hop legend Melle Mel, who helped to send "The Message" in 1982, which was the first socially conscious rap song from the new culture or, at least, the first commercially successful, conscious rap song. In 2015, just before the release of the biopic movie *Straight Outta Compton*, Ice T video-interviewed a collection of 'old school' Hip Hoppers at his *The Art of Rap* festival. He asked each of the icons sitting before his camera to recall their first impression of N.W.A. When Melle Mel was asked about the group, he confessed that he failed to understand the success of N.W.A. in the late 80s and that, almost thirty years later, he still struggled to comprehend Gangster Rap. Growing up in New York, Mel had watched his culture evolve from destructive gang life to one of constructive creativity via Hip Hop in the 1970s. 'Why go back to gang life?' he wondered. Admitting that he could be a conspiracy theorist, the pioneer pondered how Gangster Rap might be a ploy designed to make young blacks think that the worst part of their inner-city experience (selling drugs and shooting "niggas") was really the best part of it. Instead of shining light on those who rapped about these things and neglected the art of rap, Mel thought more attention should have been given to Hip Hop purists who were taking the needed time to become "experts" at emceeing, i.e. the exceptional artists who served to keep the party going instead of the senseless violence that historically preceded it.

On the West Coast, however, instead of going from gangs to partying, the trend went in the opposite direction. Original N.W.A. group member Kim Renard Nazel, better known as Arabian Prince, chronicled the reverse progression, or rather, the regression. In a 2015 interview surrounding the release of the motion picture about his former group, Nazel tells how both he and N.W.A. group member Dr. Dre were DJs on the West Coast electro music scene back in the early 80s. He goes on to explain that electro music was "starting to evolve because of our life situations in the hood . . . Early on it was about the partying and the girls and the freaks in the club, but growth in gang activity made big DJ parties unsafe."[13]

Thus, one reason East Coast rappers had a hard time artistically addressing other black and brown men as "niggas" was because they had very recently left the gang culture behind in the mid-70s. Such volatile language would not have served the purpose of perpetuating the peace which they enjoyed in those days. While on the West Coast, rappers felt that, if they were going to accurately reflect their environment, they had no choice but to talk about themselves and other minorities in expendable terms. Often, N.W.A. is credited with voicing the frustration of black youth who were dealing with the over-policing of their neighborhoods. In the advertising for the *Straight Outta Compton* movie, rapper Ice Cube states that his group's music represented a form of non-violent protest. By screaming "F*ck the Police" they could give themselves credit for being *baaad* after the fashion of Huey Newton.

N.W.A. manager and co-founder of Ruthless Records, Jerry Heller made this same comparison in 2015 as he recalled his fist impression of hearing "Boys in the Hood" one of the group's first records. "They had the rebellion of the Rolling Stones, the anger of the [Black] Panthers, and the poetry of Gil Scott Heron," he said.[14] However, it must be acknowledged that while the rap group's anger might have come from the same place as the Panthers', (i.e. feeling oppressed by an unjust social-political situation), this anger was nonetheless depicted as being unleashed on and directed at, not only police, but other "niggas" in the neighborhood whom the group saw as expendable. Thus, whereas Schooly D encountered fifteen expendable niggas on his album in 1985, and Ice T, the "Original Gangster" only one expendable nigga in 1987, N.W.A. encountered forty-four niggas on their 1988 album and twenty-eight of them were expendable.

Such gratuitous use of the word was unheard of in rap music before this time, but that did not stop other West Coast rappers from quickly following suit. However, on the East Coast things were different. Of the non-West Coast, non-Gangster Rap, Golden Era albums surveyed in the previous chapter, only EPMD had encountered an expendable nigga, or, for that matter, any type of nigga at all up to and around that time. This single instance occurred on the group's first album in 1988. EPMD member Parish Smith warned that if a group of individuals ever tried to rob him for his gold chain, he would pull out his firearm and "start spraying niggas" in self-defense. One can hear the hesitancy in his voice as he utters his first 'N' word on wax. A few years later, other East Coast rappers would confess a similar reluctance as they began to include the word in their recordings.

In 1989, EPMD cut the 'N' word out altogether, going from one instance on their first album to zero on *Unfinished Business*, their second release. While promoting the album, an interesting East Coast/West Coast connection occurred when EPMD hooked up with N.W.A. for the video of the song "The Big Payback". The cultural differences between the two coasts could not have been more obvious. As usual, the dominating subject of EPMD's song was their ability to rock the mic and lyrically demolish any competition. However, everyone knew the chief subject matter of N.W.A. was how real and how dangerous life in the streets could be, especially if members of their group were around. Car-jackings, robberies and assaults were all possibilities at any time or, retaliations for such activities.

In the video for the song "The Big Payback" EPMD group members Erick Sermon and Parish Smith are seen calling for the assistance of N.W.A. for a different type of retaliation than what the Boys in the Hood were used to. Erick and Parish rap their verses while shooting targets at a gun range during a visit to California. One sees this and immediately assumes that the situation must be serious. But what could have happened to force these East Coast rappers to take such deadly measures? It turns out that group member Erick Sermon has been ambushed and abducted by evil-doers and Parish Smith needs N.W.A.'s help to rescue him. But the evil-doers in this case are not car-thieves, gangsters, gang-bangers, or anything like what one would expect on the West Coast. The antagonists in the video are wack Emcees who have kidnapped Erick Sermon, tied him up and forced him to watch as they rock the mic in his stead. In the end, Parish Smith and N.W.A. violently burst in and save the day so that Erick can once again showcase his rap-skills in a sucka-free environment.

It is all in good, clean fun. Clearly there is not the kind of danger being intimated here that one finds in a typical N.W.A. song. No expendable niggas to speak of; just the exceptional ones with attitudes who came by for a cameo in a harmless music video in Hip Hop's first case of East meets West. When this is contrasted with Parish Smith's earlier rap lyric about "spraying niggas" with bullets for attempting to rob him of his gold chain, there are several misconceptions which must be guarded against.

Two Misconceptions

From what has been said, it could be wrongly concluded that the only reason East Coast rappers avoided the word "nigga" was because they usually only talked about rap and partying; the elementary issues for which Ice T opposed L.L. Cool J in 1987. Rappers in the East were not used to talking about everyday life in the "hood." But on the few occasions when East Coast rappers did talk about street life, *then* they were forced to use the 'N' word just like Parish Smith did on his first record in 1988.

This, however, is not the case. East Coast rappers in the mid to late 80s did talk a lot about battling 'sucka emcees.' But they also talked about being able to handle themselves in a violent scuffle, be it on the street or at a party. They used terms such as: suckas, chumps, punks, clowns, sucker-duck mother-f*ckers, f*ggots, homeboys, and brothers to identify the targets of their verbal threats and warnings. They had ample opportunity to use the 'N' word to label their foes but they rarely, if ever, did. It was not because the East Coast did not deal with real issues that they stayed away from the 'N' word, but rather, because they had lived through an era of gang wars and then were able to experience the safety of peace. For this reason, they were in no rush to go back to having their lives treated as, or treating the lives of others as expendable. They knew that their rap rhetoric was either going to reflect an image of or project an image for their culture, and they chose the latter.

Another misconception would be that the reason why the 'N' word arose in West Coast rap but not in the East is that the West Coast had gangsters, players and pimps rapping (or at least wannabe's) and the East Coast did not. It is often thought that instead of these morally questionable characters, the East Coast had a continuous stream of Conscious Rappers in the early 80s—something the West Coast knew nothing about.

This is untrue on both counts, for the West Coast had its consciousness and the East Coast had its gangsters and pimps. The previous chapter foreshadowed the way in which the Blaxploitation films of the 1970s impacted the youth who became Hip Hop heroes in the 1980s. This was true not just on the West Coast but on the East as well. Take, for instance, Antonio Hardy; arguably one of the greatest rappers of all time by any account. Born in Brooklyn in 1968, Antonio rapped his way into the spotlight taking on the name and persona of a pimp. We met him in the mid-1980s as Big Daddy Kane.

Fellow Juice Crew member and Hip Hop legend Kool G Rap commented, "[Big Daddy] Kane is what I'd call an old soul. He was like an adult from the 1970s who got zapped into the 1980s . . . [He] didn't watch a whole lot of movies of the time. He was still watching *Shaft*, *Super Fly*, and *Dolemite*. His mannerisms seemed to be like one of the ill cats of the past."[15] Kane's admiration for Blaxploitation lore and the role of the pimp could be clearly seen on his album covers and heard in his music. But he also had definite strands of consciousness in his raps, referring to himself as the "original Supreme Being" on account of his blackness. Yet, having gained this "knowledge of self" (a Five-percent religious concept which will be discussed in chapter 7) did not stop him from proclaiming that "Pimping Ain't Easy" as he and his rapping dancers bragged about profiting from sexually exploiting women.

For Big Daddy Kane, with all of his consciousness, it was still okay to be *baaad*; not just in the Black Power way, but in the same way his childhood heroes had been *baaad*. He was an East Coast rapper, he was conscious, and, in his mind, he was a pimp. On this point, one could compare Kane to West Coast rapper Too $hort who came to fame around the same time but would not have been put in the same category as any East Coast rapper.

Kane was bad in both senses of the word, and yet, his first recorded "nigga" did not come until 1990 when he made a guest appearance on Public Enemy's third album for the song "Burn Hollywood Burn." In this song, Kane, speaks as a white film maker telling black actors, "I guess I figure you can play some jiggaboo," he then uses the 'N' word in an expendable/ironic sense when he asks, "What else can a nigga do?" Ex-N.W.A. group member Ice Cube just so happened to be in the vicinity when Chuck D asked Big Daddy Kane to join him on the song. For early 90s rap fans this was a fortuitous coincidence because it was quickly decided that Cube should also be included on the track. However, it is, perhaps, no coincidence that "Burn Hollywood Burn" stands out as the most instances of Public Enemy using the 'N' word in their music up to that point.

Before this song, Public Enemy had only used the 'N' word one-and-a-half times in their previous two albums. They did not use it at all on their first album, but on their second release, lead-rapper Chuck D used the phrase "anti-nigga machine" once to refer to the prison industrial complex and the police who usher blacks into it. The 'and-a-half' time comes from Flavor Flav's use of the term "nocka" on the song "Cold Lampin'." "Nocka" was a way of saying the 'N' word without saying it, or to perhaps take some of the sting out of it. Thus, it might be easily discounted.

As for Kool G Rap, the man who charged Big Daddy Kane with being a character from a 70s Blaxploitation film, G Rap himself channeled the aura of a 1970s gangster and might be considered one of the original East Coast Gangster Rappers. And yet, as the survey above shows, when he released his first album *Road to the Riches* in 1989, just after the release of *Straight Outta Compton*, this East Coast gangster used the 'N' word zero times. But after the genie was let out of the bottle and it was clear that the 'N' word was not easily going to go back into exile, on his second album in 1992, Kool G Rap encounters 151 niggas and 149 of them were of the expendable variety. All this is to say that even though the East Coast had its gangsters and pimps beforehand, it did not see an abundance of expendable niggas until after the commercial success of N.W.A.

On the other front, the West Coast, with all of its gangsterism was not devoid of consciousness or Conscious Rap. One interesting example is the case of Tracy Lynn Curry, otherwise known as The D.O.C. Before releasing his first solo album on Ruthless records in 1989, Curry was one of the chief writers for the group N.W.A., even though he was not an official member of the group. Much of what came out of N.W.A. group member and front-man Easy E's mouth had first come through Curry's pen. So one would expect a solo album from The D.O.C. to be simply a more skillfully executed version of "Boys in the Hood." But that could not be further from what the artist actually produced. His debut album, *No One Can Do It Better* ranks, on many lists, as one of the best albums from the Golden Era of Hip Hop. Yet, the album had none of the content one would expect from a late 1980s West Coast rap album. Taking pride in this fact, The D.O.C. explained

> There was no way I was going to be confused with N.W.A., especially when my record came out ... My style was a total departure from their stuff. And here is the one point I'd like to make that really means something to me: the phenomenon was N.W.A., and when N.W.A. hit it changed the face of rap records, and everyone wanted to do the N.W.A. thing. My record came out the following year and was just as hard as *Straight Outta Compton* but with almost no cussing and none of the violence. To me, you was a real MC if you could do that. The kids wanted you to cuss, but if I could make something just as hard as N.W.A. without doing that, then to me, that was the sh*t.[16]

The D.O.C. was just as *baaad* as the Boys in the Hood but without the anti-social element on which they thrived. Having been influenced by East Coast artists such as Run DMC and Public Enemy, he seemed determined not to be "bad meaning bad but bad meaning good." On his album cover, instead of the typical gold chain around his neck, The D.O.C. wore a medallion of Africa. This was an indispensable fashion trend in the Afrocentric Hip Hop movement growing on the East Coast at that time. But, aside from these things, the N.W.A. ghost-writer also distinguished himself from his gangster peers in another way: not only did he abstain from cussing and rapping about violence, The D.O.C. went his entire album without ever invoking the 'N' word, not even once. In fact, the only time "nigga" is heard on the project is when he is joined by N.W.A. on the last song for the "Grand Finale."

Another N.W.A. affiliate, the rap-group Above the Law, is also a surprising example. The group released their debut album on Easy E's Ruthless Records in 1990. Even though the artists claimed to operate outside of the legal system, they rapped that they were "not a group promoting violence" but that "violence is something that happens in society when people are living low and they don't know where to go." Within their music, one finds bravado and threats being made against unidentified enemies; things that were becoming typical of rap music during that time. But even with all of that, listeners only encounter eight "niggas" on Above the Law's first album. Not coincidentally, seven of those encounters occur on the final song when the group is joined by members of N.W.A.

As was the case with Big Daddy Kane and Kool G. Rap in the east, there was confusion between Black Power and Blaxploitation on the West Coast. On his first album *Rhyme Pays*, in 1987, Ice T talks about convincing his friends to leave the street life alone in order to pursue a career as rap artists. He advocates carrying guns only "for protection but not to kill." In 1988, on the cover of his sophomore album *Power*, Ice T stands front and center with his DJ on his left and an almost nude woman holding a pump-action shotgun on his right. Around his neck hung an African medallion. On the album, Ice T listed his top three adversaries as "Police, Critics and Suckers." Here, the rapper advanced from one 'N' word on his first album to six on his second. It seems, the more conscious Ice T became, the more gangster he would become as well.

On his fourth album *O. G. Original Gangster*, Ice-T is introduced as "The epitome of anti-disestablishmentarianism; who embodies the entire spectrum of the urban experience and struggle [or in layman's terms] the dopest, flyest, O.G. pimp, hustler, gangster, player, hardcore motherf*cker living today." Once again, the Blaxploitation era, or error, rears its head. As a teen-ager, Ice-T had memorized the literary works of the infamous pimp-turned-author Iceburg Slim whose books were being turned into films in the 1970s. Ice-T (whose rap name is an homage to this pimp-author) along with many other inner-city youth failed to rightly distinguish between those blacks who were committed to the fight against oppression by righteous means, and those who were willing to oppress others (i.e. pimps who oppress women or drug-dealers who plague their own communities) in order to rise out of poverty. And so, for Ice-T, he could in the same breath be both a gangster-pimp and a freedom fighter.

In his earlier albums, Ice-T is unsure if he wants to rap about partying or the street life. On *Rhyme Pays* in 1987, he tells listeners that he will save the negative rap for another day. On his third album *Iceburg: Freedeom of Speech . . . Just Watch What You Say*, Ice-T ups the ante to fourteen "niggas," even as he appears more socially conscious of his responsibility as an artist. He calls others to think for themselves and to abandon self-destructive and community crippling behaviors such as gang violence and selling or using drugs. But by the time of *O.G. Original Gangster*, in 1991, Hip Hop had fully embraced both the nigga who was "bad meaning good" and the one who was bad for no good reason. These two versions of the bad nigga had been conflated into one identity. Thus, by the time of his fourth album, Ice-T had grown comfortable enough to encounter a total of ninety-one "niggas" on the project. This comfort came, partially because of the intentional effort Ice-T made to draw attention to the exceptional nature of some niggas, especially himself as he rapped on the song "Straight Up Nigga"

> I'm up stand-up nigga. A low down nigga gets hype but I'm not a nigga of that type. . . Not a watermelon, chitlin eatin' nigga from down south but a nigga that'll smack the taste out your mouth . . . A steak and lobster eatin' . . . corporate jet glidin, limousine riding, filthy rich nigga.

For those African Americans who would attempt to reprimand him for taking ownership of the 'N' word, he reveals to them the irony that in America "they're looked upon as a nigga just like" him, whether they call themselves "niggas" or not. The lesson that Ice-T seems to have learned and wants to teach is: if you're going to be a nigger anyway (however ironic it might be), don't be an expendable one; be an exceptional one.

One cannot end a discussion on the West Coast and Conscious rap without mentioning two names. First is the artist Paris, who released his debut album, *The Devil Made Me Do It*, in 1990. As the Hip Hop extension of the Black Power Movement, Paris rapped with what he called, "Panther Power" and set himself apart from both early 80s East Coast rap and 1990 West Coast artists. He asks, "Remember back when good rap was just a cool dance hit even though it wasn't sayin' sh*t?" In another song he advises, "If you want to dance" then he is not the artist for you. Hip Hop music for him is about cultural leadership and so, "When you're ready for the brother who leads" then you can play his songs.

When his music is played, what does one find? The casting off of ignorance and the birth of consciousness. Paris wants to see all blacks in America unite as an army that will eventually wrest from the government all that has been withheld from his people. He violently warns the police that blacks have had enough of their brutality, noting that blacks can be brutal too. But, he explains, he's "not N.W.A." and doesn't make "rhymes that say how ignorant brothers act now-a-days." This sounds very similar to East Coast, Conscious rapper KRS One who, in 1988, rapped

> Some Emcees be talkin' and talkin' trying to show how black people are walkin'/ but I don't walk that way to portray or reinforce stereotypes of the day/ like all my brothers eat chicken and watermelon/ talk broken English and drug-sellin'

Like KRS, Paris saw that Gangster Rap was not simply reflecting the urban reality, but rather, it was projecting a negative image for the culture to follow. But he was determined to project something different. Often, what sets the conscious rapper apart is his willingness to teach and sometimes, even to preach. In the process of delivering his sermonic songs, Paris makes use of the word "nigga" a total of three times on his first album. Two of these uses are the expendable nigga, used in an effort to shame his listeners out of certain ignorant behaviors; and one is a reference to the exceptional nigga. Paris takes a stand against drug-dealers in the neighborhood, threatening to violently punish them for selling poison in the community. Chapter six will seek to explain why popular rap has gone away from speaking out against the drug dealer to largely advocating, or at the least, excusing this type of criminality.

The other name which must be mentioned in connection with West Coast Hip Hop and Conscious rap is that of Tupac Shakur. Tupac's life and career is an almost perfect metaphor for the development of Hip Hop, both east and west. Shakur was born and raised on the East Coast in Harlem, New York in 1971. Both of his parents were members of the Black Panther Party and many of his relatives were active in militant, Black Power, anti-establishment groups. As Hip Hop entered into its Golden Era, Shakur was entering his teenage years and began to hone his rap skills. Soon after, he would move to Baltimore where his New York flare set him apart as the best rapper in his school, among his many other talents. Then, before he could complete high school, his family relocated to the West Coast, just outside of San Francisco, California, around the same time that N.W.A. caused the axis of Hip Hop to tilt toward the west.

In 1991, at the age of 20, Tupac released his first album *2Pacalypse NOW* and, just like with Paris, it was as if the Black Power Movement had extended to Hip Hop through his music. He begins the album with a call to "Niggas" and in his tone, one can hear the double and even triple entandre. Did he mean to shame blacks away from ignorance or to highlight the irony that his people were still seen as expendable niggers in America? Was he simply referring to those to whom he feels endeared, i.e. to "my niggas?" Or did he literally mean to refer to, at least, some blacks as expendable? On the album, Tupac has two clearly defined enemies: in some cases it is other blacks but in other cases it is the police. Perceptively he tells his African American listeners that "the war on drugs is a war on you and me." He understood that African Americans did not have to be drug dealers to be targets of police harassment.

On the album, Tupac warns of violence, not for violence's sake but says he is "giving [police] a reason to claim that I'm violent." Since he is being perceived and treated as a threat, 'why not finally earn the title that is being assigned to him?' he figured. Just two years prior, in an interview with Dee Barnes, rapper Ice Cube was asked why his group chose the name Niggaz Wit Attitude. His response was "because it sounded scary" and they "wanted to scare a lot of people."[17] But the fear was already there. Since the days of the 1915 racially charged silent-film *Birth of A Nation*, white America had been concocting ways to depict freed blacks as threats to be feared. And, thanks to this fear, the need for blacks to be politically and socially controlled was plain to all. Artists like Tupac were simply playing the part that blacks had been asked to play for decades. But now, they were taking control of their own narrative. They would determine for themselves how and why they were to be feared. On *2Pacalypes Now*, Shakur tells white America, "I am America's nightmare. I am what you made me; the hate and the evil that you gave me." This is reminiscent of Paris who, one year earlier rapped asking, "Who's to blame for the hate that hate made?" Whether it was self-hate or hate of the white-other, these rappers knew that their negative emotion was a response to racism, not the cause of it.

Thirty years before Paris and Tupac, James Baldwin told white America, "You invented the Nigga. You invested me with its attributes but, in actuality, it reflects you. I give you your problem back." But these

West Coast rappers, along with the likes of Chuck D and KRS One on the East Coast, were those who unleashed verbal tirades against police and the establishment. This was the Hip Hop generation's way of giving America back the Niggas it had created. There was now a culture of young people who were willing to proclaim along with Tupac, "I just don't give a f*ck" in the face of institutionalized racism. America was going to have to deal with its worst nightmare, conscious Niggas Wit Attitude.

With all of his consciousness, Tupac made eighty-five references to "niggas" on his first album. But like Ice-T and others in the past, an effort was made to take the venom out of the nasty name and to inject it with new meaning. Tupac's was a clever attempt to turn the term into an acronym meaning Never Ignorant Getting Goals Accomplished. He even titled his second album *Strictly for My N.I.G.G.A.Z...* in an effort to drive home his point of view. Still, on his first album, when the acronym was introduced, sixty of the eighty-five niggas encountered were not *N.I.G.G.A.Z...* but instead, were of the expendable variety.

Chicago rapper Common, in his song "I Used to Love Her" chronicled the way in which Hip Hop traveled from the East to the West Coast and embraced Gangster Rap. Something similar can be said of Tupac Shakur. Progressively, as the West Coast gave way to the bad nigga who was bent on being bad for no good reason, Tupac took on the persona of a "thug" and gave a voice to violence while offering less expression of the consciousness with which he entered the rap world. Then, sadly, other thugs were willing to treat him like one of the expendable niggas he rapped so much about in the mid-90s. As a result, Hip Hop lost a leader in Las Vegas, Nevada on September 13, 1996 when Shakur was shot to death.

All of this is to show that the West Coast, with its gangsters and pimps, did not lack consciousness, and the East Coast, with all of its consciousness, was not without gangsters and pimps. The combined examples of Black Power and Blaxploitation had set a confusing standard of what it meant to be "bad" for rappers in both regions. And yet, up until the early 1990s, the coast which had ended its gang activity in the 70s was uncomfortable with the 'N' word, while the coast which was growing in its gang activity in the 80s easily embraced the artistic depiction of expendable niggas; niggas who were not just expendable in the eyes of police or the political system, but in the eyes of other African Americans as well.

5

Navigating the Strength of Strawman Arguments

"When N.W.A. hit, everybody wanted to do the N.W.A. thing," said The D.O.C. But, technically, not everyone wanted to be niggas with attitude or rap about treating other blacks like expendable niggas. Cultural leaders on the East Coast put up a fight, though the West was more easily won to the new trend. On the *Straight Outta Compton* album, Ice Cube asked, "Do I look like a mother-f*ckin role model?" Before the mind has had enough time to answer the rhetorical question, he continues with, "To a kid lookin' up to me, life ain't nothin' but b*tches and money. Cuz I'm the type of nigga that's built to last." It was important for him to point out that he and his companions were not just niggas, rather, they were the exceptional type.

For other young blacks who were tired of being viewed and treated as expendables, this seemed to be an effective way to distinguish one's self and rise above the pack. Thus, the nameless, faceless "nigga" became a common feature of rap music that followed the N.W.A. format. This is because the expendable nigga is the perfect strawman. A 'strawman argument' is when a person voices the weakest version of his opponent's view only to, then, quickly and easily tear the view down. This is an unfair debate tactic but it does two things: it gives the impression that both sides of an issue have been fairly vocalized; and it gives the appearance that the one who has torn down the weak argument must have had the stronger position and, therefore, has won the debate.

By filling one's music with an abundance of expendable niggas, rappers have an endless supply of strawmen whom they can destroy and, thereby, be seen as victorious. One can demolish a nameless, faceless nigga—shoot him, sleep with more females than him, sleep with his girlfriend, or get more money than him; and because he is only a figment of rap fiction, listeners can never fact-check to see if this expendable nigga has ever really been demolished, shot, or in any way outdone by the rapper who claims to have bested him.

The one who uses the expendable nigga in his music this way can disclaim, "No actual niggas were hurt during the recording of this album." At the same time, this rapper can label himself "exceptional," lifting his self higher by standing on a pile of expendable black bodies. This methodology caught on with many West Coast and Southern rap artists almost immediately, but not as fast in the East.

Consider just a few cases from the survey charted in chapter three. The Geto Boys (hailing from Texas) released their first album *Making Trouble* in 1988, just before the release of *Straight Outta Compton*. For all of their musical mischief, the rap group did not feel the liberty or need to use one single "nigga" on the album. But in 1989, they came back with *Grip It! On Another Level*. And they did indeed take it to another level, going from zero "niggas" on their first album to forty-three on their second. The 2 Live Crew released their first album in 1986 and, like the Geto Boys, utilized a total of zero "niggas" on the project. But when they came back in 1988, just after the release of *Straight Outta Compton*, 2 Live Crew could count sixty-nine "niggas" on their second release. Five of these were dependable, one exceptional and the rest, expendable. Interestingly, the group even gives a 'shout out' to Compton on the album.

The influence of N.W.A. is undeniable as it relates to the practice of using expendable niggas as strawmen to build one's reputation, especially for those who began their rap careers after 1988. Take, for example, the case of Percy Miller aka Master P. Originally from New Orleans, Louisiana, Master P moved to Oakland,

California to complete his college education in the late 1980s. On the song "Gangsta, Gangsta" Ice Cube challenged the idea that he could be seen as a role model. But in 1991, on Master P's first album, *Get Away Clean*, it becomes clear that Ice Cube has, indeed, mentored many young men through his music.

The first words heard on Master P's album are the same words heard initially from Cube's legendary group: "You are now about to witness the strength of street knowledge." The impact of the group looms large over the rest of the album also. The musical production sounds like a hurried effort to imitate N.W.A.'s Dr. Dre. The subject matter is similar and yet even more brazen. When Ice Cube rapped about being a "gangster," at the end of the song he ends up "dressed in the county blues" (a prison uniform). But Master P envisions himself escaping police capture and getting away clean when breaking the law. However, there is one thing that he does completely share with Ice Cube. On the album, Master P proudly proclaimed that for him, "Life ain't nothin' but b*tches and money!" As seen in this artistic imitation, rappers cannot escape the fact that their lyrics have tremendous influence over others.

On his debut album, Master P. spoke of "niggas" forty-one times: six of these were dependable, seven exceptional and the remaining twenty-eight, expendable. As was stated at the end of chapter three, the increase of the expendable nigga in rap music made it necessary for there be an increase of exceptional niggas in order to set oneself apart. Both the West and the South exhibit this early on.

Not So Fast

Rappers on the East Coast were hesitant and, in many cases, resistant to the idea of proliferating the 'N' word through their art. As the above survey results show, several Golden-era artists who had released "nigga-less" albums before the dawn of *Straight Outta Compton* continued on, unpersuaded by the new trend. Among these were Big Daddy Kane and the rap duo EPMD who excluded the word after using it once on their first album. Other noteworthy cases include that of Rakim, who did not use the "N" word until his fourth album *Don't Sweat the Technique* in 1992. When he eventually did, Rakim used the word three times and all three uses occurred in the same song "Know the Ledge" which was originally recorded for the soundtrack to the movie *Juice*. One can deduce that he only used the "N" word to tell the story of one of the characters from the film, since it is missing from his three previous albums.

KRS One used the word for the first time on wax on his third album in 1989. On *Ghetto Music: The Blueprint of Hip Hop*, this Conscious Rapper made use of the term "nigga" twice. One of these instances was in the mouth of a police officer who had run the rapper down with a patrol car. The other occurred on the same song, "Bo, Bo, Bo" when, because of his willingness to talk back to police, KRS believes he is seen as an "uppity nigga," i.e. a black person who thinks he is exceptional when he is really still just an expendable nigga. But, despite what was happening on the West Coast, KRS still had not used his raps to label any of his own people "nigga."

In 1990, this same Conscious Rapper upped the ante going from two to eight "niggas" on his fourth album *Edutainment*. Here, the term was used to illustrate the way black radio DJs shun rap music. KRS compared these media gatekeepers to "house-niggas" who were more loyal to the white master (corporate America) than to the field-nigga (rappers). On the same album, the rapper, also known as The Teacher, claims that because of his metaphysical approach to life (explained in chapter 7) he is able to rule on the East Coast and "even in Compton." He is aware of the differences between him and N.W.A. but believes that his intellect and consciousness will guide him to success even in Hip Hop's Gangster-prone, western region.

There were other examples of East Coast resistance to the new trend. When the biopic movie *Straight Outta Compton* was set to release in 2015, the internet was overrun with memes boasting "Strait Outta _____" spoof names. Web-users could not wait to fill in the blank with their humorous captions. But this trend was twenty-five years behind the first "meme" to put a spin on the title. New York native rap group The Jungle Brothers released their groundbreaking debut *Straight Out the Jungle* just three months after N.W.A. released the *Straight Outta Compton* album in August of 1988. On it, the Brothers wasted no time setting themselves apart from the trends of the day. "I don't wear no gold around my neck," they rapped, "just black medallions." Offering their social commentary on West Coast gang-life, they opined "men killing men because of a color . . . in this lifetime I've seen nothing dumber." The group is credited with helping to birth the Afrocentric movement within Hip Hop. Accordingly, the Jungle Brothers encountered zero niggas on their first album.

Another credit to The Jungle Brothers is that they introduced the world to the rapper Q-tip from the group A Tribe Called Quest. The "Tribe" (for short) powerfully demonstrates the East Coast's struggle as it relates to using the 'N' word in rap. The group is known for its fusion of jazz and Hip Hop as well as being a part of the Native Tongues, a collection of other jazzy, Hip Hop, afro-centric artists including The Jungle Brothers, De La Soul and more. In 1990, a year-and-a-half after Q-tip was featured on *Straight Out the Jungle*, A Tribe Called Quest released their debut album *People's Instinctive Travels and Paths of Rhythm*. The album made no, zero, mention of "niggas." In 1991 the Tribe released their second album, *Low End Theory* in which they lyrically encountered one single, solitary "nigga."

However, on the group's third album *Midnight Marauders*, Q-tip confessed his moral dilemma with using the word which had taken over rap music in 1993. This take-over seemed inevitable because, as he says, "little kids grow up hearing it" and "a whole bunch of niggas put it in their rhymes." But, the rapper admitted that he "starts to flinch as [he] tries not to say it." He reasons that the word has been used as a term of endearment and so, maybe it was okay to use it. As a result, Tribe was able to keep up with Hip Hop's trend and use the 'N' word seventy-two times on their third album – twice to speak of exceptional niggas and seventy times to refer to expendable niggas (mostly using it for its shaming or ironic effect). Yet, surprisingly, it was used zero times to speak of dependable niggas, even though Q-tip had sanctioned it as a term of endearment.

One last example will do to show the creative ways in which East Coast rappers struggled to respond to the growing trend of becoming exceptional by disposing of expendable niggas. In 1990, the rapper King Sun released his debut album *Righteous but Ruthless*. Immediately one thinks of N.W.A. and Easy E's West Coast record empire, Ruthless Records. Was King Sun aiming to make a point about what it really means to be a *baaad* nigga? Was he, in effect, saying that it was okay to be ruthless as long as one was committed to being righteous at the same time? This would mirror what rap-group Public Enemy stated on their first album in 1987 when Chuck D rapped, "I don't break in stores but I break all laws" and warned, "I'm not a law obeyer so tell your mayor." This is a throwback to the historic "bad nigga."

Like many Golden Era, East Coast Hip Hop artists, King Sun's sense of righteousness flowed from his 5

Percent Nation religious teachings. He states that he has studied 120 (explained in chapter 7) and therefore knows what it means to "be black." He encourages his ethnic brothers and sisters to "be civilized" since they are "no longer the people who were bought and sold" as slaves. It is time for them to "snap out of the negative." The album begins with a sample of Richard Pryor asking the question, "Have any of you ever been to Africa?" Chapter two of this book discussed how Pryor returned from his journey to the "Mother-land" with a commitment to never again call another black man "nigga." Perhaps this is the reason why King Sun does not utter the 'N' word at all on his debut album. And yet, the word is heard no less than twenty-two times on the project. How does he manage to pull this off; to stay righteous while at the same time keep up with the day's trend of violently disposing of niggas?

All twenty-two instances of the 'N' word occur on the song "Soft Shoe Booty" where King Sun displays his ability to lyrically crush his rhyming competitors. Figuratively, he kills the competition by erecting the perfect strawman – the expendable nigga. But rather than use the word himself, the rapper goes to the pros to get the job done. The song's chorus samples and repeats N.W.A.'s opening line "Witness the strength" along with Ice Cube's voice lamenting, "Just another nigga dead" from the extended version of the song "Straight Outta Compton." Thus King Sun was able to remain righteous while still giving the impression that he was ruthless. Thanks to Ice Cube's voice, this East

Coast artist was able to present himself as exceptional at the expense of lesser-talented, nameless, faceless, unverifiable niggas.

No Harm, No Foul

As the survey in Chapter 3 shows, in the first half of the 1990s the East Coast began to rival the rest of the country in the amount of expendable niggas being depicted in rap music. Many rappers of the time asked, 'What's the big deal? No one is really being hurt.' For instance, in his song "Lethal Weapon" Ice-T disagrees with those who claim that his lyrics are promoting violence. He sees his music as "entertainment like *Terminator* on T.V." If Arnold Schwarzenegger can fire automatic weapons into cities full of human beings, why can't a rapper leave fifty-five niggas outlined in police chalk on an album? This exact argument and example has been used by countless rappers since it was first put forth by the Original Gangster. But it lacks cogency for several reasons.

1) It fails to recognize the race-based nature of using the expendable nigga as Hip Hop's strawman. Imagine if the *Terminator* movies were about a robot being sent back in time to kill a particular African American woman who was going to give birth to a black man who would save the entire black race; and in the movie series, the robot only killed black people; if this were the case, no one would accept the claim that 'it's just entertainment so what's the big

deal?' What's more, if the robot had assumed the image of a black man in order to pull of this genocide, movie-goers would wonder what kind of self-hate software program had been written into the murderous machines operating system

Where rap music is concerned, the only ones being depicted as worthy of death, are niggas. It would immediately strike the mind as racist if rappers were to single out whites or Asians for the same violence that is presently reserved for expendable niggas. What needs to be considered is this: even if Gangster/Thug/Drill/Trap-rap music is just entertainment, isn't it racist entertainment if the only ones being targeted for destruction are black people?

It has been argued that the reason why black rappers target other blacks in their music is because many of these artists have grown up in racially segregated neighborhoods, and so they are only used to seeing other blacks. Had they grown up around whites they would likely be targeting whites too and this would be reflected in the music. But the sociology is deeper than that. On the title-track to his 1991 album *Amerikkka's Most Wanted*, Ice Cube depicts a black criminal's rude awakening when he leaves the 'hood' to expand his crime-spree to the suburbs. He complains, "I think back when I was robbing my own kind, the police didn't pay it no mind. But when I start robbing the white folks, now I'm in the [penitentiary] with the soap-on-a-rope."

America has made one thing clear to him: his people are expendable, but whites are not. Therefore, black criminals cannot treat the two races in the same way. It is this unjust version of justice that teaches black criminals that it is safer to target their own people with ill intent. On the album, Ice Cube utters fifty-two "niggas" and thirty-four of them refer to the expendable kind. This is not simply entertainment. It is internalized racism; or, at least, an album which bemoans the social system that has led to this internalization.

2) Ice-T's *Terminator* example fails to fully appreciate the social conditioning involved in such a lop-sided presentation of the "bad nigga" as entertainment. From both sides of the fence – black and white, citizen and police – Hip Hop will have to own up to its part in helping to create, or in some cases, reinforce negative stereotypes of black men as criminals on the one hand and as expendable on the other.

It is hard to escape the claim of hypocrisy when a group of African Americans scream "Black Lives Matter" when a black person is killed by a police officer and yet, no outcry is heard when parents drive through the city with toddlers packed in the car, listening to the day's hottest rapper report on how many niggas he has been able to literally or figuratively reduce to nothing. Of course it is not the same thing: in the one case black people are actually dying whereas in the other, it is only being portrayed artistically. But if a child has been taught to devalue black life from the time he or she is young, we cannot be surprised when the same child has very little respect for the lives of other blacks by the time he or she reaches adulthood.

We must ask, 'what role does this entertainment play in the way young blacks have come to see and value themselves and their peers?' Why is there such outrage when a police officer takes a life while attempting to do his or her job, but almost no emotional reaction when black on black crime is reported? Where does this numbness come from?

In 2014, the rapper J Cole began to fill the enormous weight that lay upon entertainers in the rap genre. Consider this excerpt from an interview conversation between he and radio personality Angie Martinez

Angie: Isn't it amazing what you can do with music?

J Cole: It's amazing . . . It's the most powerful thing.

Angie: It's not always because people don't always use it that way . . . but when they use it that way. . .

J Cole: It's even just as powerful when they don't use it [that way], it's just the wrong type of power. We don't notice it cuz we can't see but it's just as powerful; it's just using power the wrong way.

Angie: Does that scare you at all?

J Cole: Definitely! Absolutely. When I was young it didn't matter. Now I'm like sick . . . I like some of these song too. I like a lot of them. But it's like when I really think I'm just like, I'm getting sick; I'm tired. It's not cool no more. We been singing the same songs for thirty years. These dudes is portraying a lifestyle that a) they probably didn't live and b) even if you did, you don't no more but you still trying to milk us and feed us this and sell us this so that some kid somewhere...[18]

With those words, the rappers eye's got wide, as if mimicking an impressionable youngster who is being wowed by the gangster lifestyle portrayed by popular rappers. He did not finish his statement but his point was clear; what Ice-T called "entertainment" thirty years ago has become nauseating to those aware of the impact of the music in the neighborhoods where rap lyrics are lived out.

If 'Black Lives Matter' then they do not only matter when taken by police. They also matter when portrayed as expendable or criminal in cultural art. To J Cole's point, thirty years of depicting the bad nigga who is bad for no good reason has not helped to change the nation's perception of African Americans. "You want to treat me like a criminal? Okay, then I'll act like one." This was the social commentary behind N.W.A. But at what point does the culture pause and ask how well this strategy is working to better police-community relations? And if it is not working, is it time for a new strategy?

This last question came to the fore in 2014 after the death of Mike Brown, the unarmed Missouri teen whose deadly encounter with a white police officer sparked the "Hands Up, Don't Shoot" protests which launched the Black Lives Matter movement into the national conversation. As the tension and attention rose concerning the issue, a host of popular rappers came together at the behest of Compton rapper The Game to record the song "Don't Shoot." On the chorus, a group of children's voices sing a plea to police, "God ain't put us on the earth to get murdered . . . It's murder; don't point your weapons at me." This was a drastic difference from what a group of Compton rappers had to say to police thirty years ago.

Over a dozen artist appeared on the song with The Game, but only rapper Yo Gotti took the liberty to use the 'N' word, proclaiming, "I know how niggas feel out there" in Ferguson, Missouri. Angry that the media would focus more on the looting than the protests, portraying blacks "like we some animals," Gotti shouts out N.W.A. and ends his verse with "F*ck the Police." The other artist on the song were no less angry, but managed to find a host of different words in order to refer to themselves and other minorities, such as: Son, Brother, Boy, Teens, Black Men, Boss, People, The Lost and Mother F*ckers, Most importantly, they used these – Emmett Till, Ezell Ford, Sean Bell, Trayvan Martin, Mike Brown – names.

Temple University professor of 'Hip Hop & Black Culture' Timothy Welbeck released a rap song entitled "Nobody" around the same time as "Don't Shoot." In his song, Welbeck used some of these same names in order to make the point that, to black youth, the message seems to be, 'You're nobody until somebody kills you.' But in light of the present discussion it seems that the message is a bit more disturbing: black lives matter and black victims get a name, not simply when they are murdered but, when they are murdered by police, or at least, by non-blacks. However, when a black person is the killer there is no outrage. The victims are simply nameless, faceless expendable niggas in the song of some rapper.

This irony was not lost on Agape, a young artist who delivered an acapella rap video in response to The Game's "Don't Shoot" song. In it, he challenged the artists on the song to care as much about black life when it is lost at the hands of other blacks and not to celebrate the loss of this life in their music. Poetically, he asks, "What happened to black pride when [Huey] Newton and truth died this music is true lies that they got you believin'/ the new 'Black Power' is the act of a coward lettin' them [bullets] shower like your brother's not a human being."

This is a powerful point. Thirty years of treating Blaxploitation as if it were Black Power has had disastrous results. The message communicated is that blacks can only become exceptional at the expense of other blacks. This bizarre logic was borne out in a telling interview with Atlanta based rapper Young Jeezy conducted by legendary, lady rapper-turned-radio personality Monie Love in 2006. Around that time, the rapper Nas had pronounced Hip Hop dead and had even released an album titled to that effect. This was after it had become clear that the New York born culture had relocated to the nation's south. Many first generation Hip Hoppers had a problem with what they saw as southern, "uneducated" and "undignified" representations of African Americans being promoted as Hip Hop.

Nas, by this time in his career, was ready to commit to a more conscious style of rap, something he both flirted and struggled with in his heyday. But Young Jeezy challenged Nas' diagnosis that Hip Hop had died. Rather, he said, it was simply seeing a new day. And if

Hip Hop did, indeed, die in the north it was immediately resurrected in the south. Monie Love responded with a Hip Hop history lesson and gave her explanation of why both she and Nas could say that Hip Hop was dead. "The original concept of Hip Hop is all different forms," she told him. "It's not just talking about one area of Hip Hop in as far as struggles, street hustling and coming up, which is a respected factor." Notice here that Monie Love's issue was not that Jeezy and others were rapping about flooding black communities with drugs. This, was "a respected factor." Her problem was that the other forms, such as the consciousness that Nas was calling for, were not getting the same light as was street hustling. Her problem was that only the unrighteous version of the bad nigga was succeeding in Hip Hop art.

Even though both versions of the bad nigga had become culturally acceptable, in reality, only the one who was willing to be bad for no good reason was being considered 'good.' Meanwhile the original bad nigga who was simply willing to stand up against unjust laws, to fight for equality and promote consciousness had become marginalized. In the same radio interview, Young Jeezy went on to invalidate Nas by asking, "Nas ain't no street nigga. Do Nas bust his guns? Has Nas been on the block [selling drugs]? Do Nas have street credibility? Is any of Nas' homies in the feds [federal penitentiary]?"[19]

If this is the litmus test for what it means to be an "exceptional," "straight up" or "bad" nigga then, once again, Ice-T's "entertainment" explanation goes out the window. It is not enough to rap about it, one must be about it. Not only that, but it becomes clear that there is a need to re-evaluate whether "street hustling and coming up" ought to be a "respected factor" or should these be rejected as relics from the days of Blaxploitation. Excusing the ethic of the unrighteous bad nigga stands in the way of progress and any true movement that seeks to affirm black lives or black power.

6

Navigating the Highs and Lows of Hierarchy

"I'm coming up the rough side of the mountain. I'm doing my best to make it in," goes the chorus to an old Gospel song. The word gospel is originally a Greek word which means 'good news.' However, many theologians would argue that a rough road to the mountain-top, leading to uncertain results based on the best efforts of an imperfect human-being is not really 'good news' at all. If at the top of the mountain lies the entrance into heaven, one would hope for a more promising route than this. But it is well-known that many spiritual songs, having originated in the black church, do not only have spiritual implications but social ones as well. The mountain-top can figuratively represent any number of progressive developments for the advancement of colored people.

During the Civil Rights era, Dr. Martin Luther King Jr. used the biblical imagery of Moses leading the children of Israel to the Promised Land as a metaphor for finally achieving racial equality and social justice in America. He declared, "I've been to the mountain-top . . . I've looked over and I've seen the Promised Land. I may not get there with you, but we as a people will get to the Promised Land." He felt in his soul that he himself would not make it. The way forward was too fraught with danger. But the good news was that others would be able to make it because of the leadership and sacrifice of this one man.

Whether the mountain-top or the Promised Land is a reference to an actual heaven, a divinely blessed geographical area or simply a metaphor for achieving the heavenly bliss of social equality, it is not at all good news if the way to reaching the destination is a treacherous journey up the rough side of a mountain. And it is even worse news if, after doing the best one can, there is still no guarantee that he or she will ever be able to actually reach the goal.

Climbing Mount Maslow

African Americans currently find themselves stratified at varying levels of ascension on the journey up the mountain of equality. Some feel trapped at the base of the mount. Very few make it to the top. But it is not just black people who are struggling to climb. Financial status is used to identify the wealthy as 'upper-class' and the poor as 'lower-class.' This is the prevailing hierarchical system in America where the goal of many is simply to make it into the middle-class. But there is one hierarchy in particular which goes a long way toward explaining why many individuals often remain at the lower levels and also, why very few make it to the top. The hierarchy itself is not responsible for this trend, but the way in which it is approached often produces these results.

In 1943, psychologist Abraham Maslow introduced what he called a "hierarchy of needs" which drive human behavior. At the very bottom of the hierarchy lie the physiological needs, i.e. mankind's most basic compulsions. Take a moment to study figure below. At first glance, it seems to make complete sense that if a person cannot breathe or if one goes too long without food or water, then he or she cannot spend too much time focusing on the higher needs of love and belonging. From this, it is argued that the way we operate as human-beings is to meet each level of the lower needs and then, progressively, to ascend the mount in order to obtain the higher needs.

In *The Death of Hip Hop, Marriage & Morals*, the first book in this present series, I critiqued the bottom-up direction of Maslow's hierarchy. While contrasting the bottom-up approach with a top-down method, attention was drawn to the ways in which first-

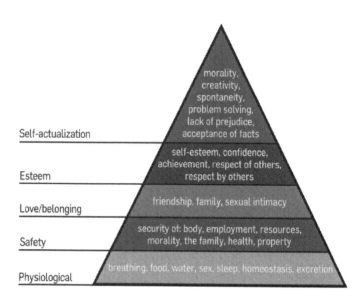

generation, Northeast Hip Hop differed from the representation of Hip Hop which sprang from the South around the turn of the millennium. One of the chief differences was that much of Golden Era, Northeast Hip Hop followed the historical trajectory of W.E.B. Dubois in believing that the most talented and intellectually gifted African Americans within the culture had an obligation to teach the rest. While Hip Hop artists from the nation's South tended to reflect the mindset of Dubois' opponent, Booker T. Washington, who believed that the best way for blacks to advance in American society was make their chief aim economic stability, and to cease striving to be able to exercise their constitutional rights or demanding to be treated with basic human dignity. These things would come, not overnight through activism, but over time through the accumulation of wealth as whites and blacks worked toward that which was mutually beneficial, financially speaking.

Dubois was concerned about *The Souls of Black Folk* and believed that his people sorely needed an education in history and morality; in the deep issues which ancient societies held as the bedrock of civilization. Because of the effects of slavery, African Americans, he felt, were playing 'catch-up' with the rest of the world in these matters. For him, self-respect and self-worth would not come from amassing dollars but from accumulating and applying the wisdom of the ages to the current situation. On the other hand, Washington wanted whites to help black people rise *Up From Slavery* and suggested that Negroes should do what Abraham Maslow would later lay out in his hierarchy, i.e. worry about the lower levels of need, especially safety and securing their economic security, and *then* only slowly, over the course of time, worry about things like self-esteem and suffrage, i.e. the higher levels of the hierarchy.

Started from the Bottom

It is a materialist view of the world that puts physiological needs first and portrays the 'soul' or 'self' as a by-product or concept which comes as a result of achieving the lower levels. But if this were how humans really operate, think about what it would mean. According to Maslow's hierarchy, a person does not, indeed cannot, be too concerned with creativity until his or her lower needs have been met. In such a world, the phrase "starving artist" would not exist because the starving individual would have no creativity to speak of. He would not be motivated to reach that level. However, in real life, the opposite is true. Often the rich, successful artist who has lost his hunger is the one who no longer digs deep to draw on the creativity which catapulted him to fame in the first place.

Consider, also, what this bottom-up approach to the hierarchy means for the question of *morality*. If this important facet of societal and personal life is left off down at the lowest level, then a person cannot be harshly judged for performing immoral acts as long as their needs remain unmet. Robbery and theft, selling drugs, selling one's body, selling the body of someone else (as a pimp does) – all of these would normally be seen as immoral to some degree. But if a woman is struggling to feed herself and her children, can we blame her for acting immorally in order to get food? And can we blame her pimp if he, too, has a family to feed and no other way to feed them? Until the lower level is secured, we should not expect him to act in a moral way. This is the danger of approaching the hierarchy from the bottom – going up the rough side of the mountain.

The road to the top gets even rougher when the legal system is designed to single out and penalize some individuals for acting immorally but not others. Those who are more aggressively policed, arrested, charged, prosecuted, convicted, sentenced and thereby stigmatized as criminals and locked out of society in the most meaningful of ways, will be forced to struggle at the lower levels of the hierarchy. Disproportionately, this applies to African Americans and people of color in the United States. There is hypocrisy here. Not only are minorities more harshly penalized for acting immorally while struggling at the lower levels but, through institutionalized racism, whites have been able to do some of the most immoral things to others while giving themselves credit for being the most civilized and cultured individuals in society. These acts have escaped the "immoral" label because they have been committed against those who are seen as non-humans, against "niggers." Meanwhile, many whites who have committed or been complicit in these acts, or who have benefited from them via what is commonly called 'white privilege' have pictured themselves as resting at the top of the hierarchy with their sense of morality remaining fully intact. This moral indemnity is one of the advantages of using the 'N' word to dehumanize ones victims.

We can now tie this discussion in with the previous chapters. Historically, the "Nigger" was a myth used by whites to convince themselves of their own exceptional nature; that they deserved to live in luxury at the expense of others. They could hold blacks down at the bottom of the hierarchy, struggling to secure their basic needs: forced to subsist on the most unfit allocations of food, rest, and lodging; having no sense of safety from tyrannical slave masters; no sense of belonging and intimacy, knowing that their families and communities could be ripped apart and undone at any moment. Despite these struggles, it is amazing that blacks have achieved any sense of having a soul. And yet, an undeniable product of the African American slavery experience is the many "soulful" creations, ranging from music to food, dating from that time.

"Nigger" was used to deny the undeniable, i.e. the souls of black folk, and to treat spiritual people as though they were only material. The people guilty of this oppression used the word in order to prop themselves up as exceptional even while they did the most immoral things to be able to maintain their status. By keeping the 'N' word alive today, even if whites are not allowed to say it, the myth of the nigger remains alive and well. Black Americans, themselves, can be just as guilty as whites of employing the term in order to prop themselves up as exceptional at someone else's expense.

Hip Hop and the Hierarchy

Much of modern, popular rap music can be used to show how Maslow's hierarchy relates to all three uses of the 'N' word, especially when going from the bottom to the top. This will help to explain, at a socio-psychological level, the stratified depiction of black lives – some seeming to matter while others do not.

Expendable Level

At the two lowest levels of the hierarchy (physiological needs & safety) we meet the expendable nigga. Here there is competition to secure one's basic needs and anyone who stands in the way is expendable. Notice, however, that safety (whether it be for oneself or for others) does not become a concern, and neither does morality, until the very first level of needs is met. One thinks of the lyrics to the song "What We Do" by Philadelphia rapper Freeway, when addressing this level.

Born Leslie Pridgen, the artist took his rap name from the famed 1980s drug trafficker "Freeway" Ricky Ross. In the song, the rapper boasts about selling drugs and violently attacking other black men because of his own hunger and compulsion to secure his basic needs. But he does not see himself as being alone in this practice. After rapping about pulling a gun on someone during a robbery he asserts, "If you're from the hood I know you feel me." During the song's brief intermissions, Freeway's musical mentor, rapper Jay Z encourages him to "keep going" as the chorus sings "even though what we do is wrong." On the one hand, Freeway knows it is wrong to rob, but on the other hand, instinctively he feels that he has a moral right to be wrong if the only way he can feed himself and those in his care is by doing that which is immoral. Listeners are asked to ignore his immorality on account of his circumstances. And, according to Maslow's hierarchy, perhaps they should. For it seems the issue of morality is the privilege of the well-fed only. It does not come into play when one is struggling at the very bottom.

Confusion about morality at this level is not simply a modern, inner-city struggle. One can go as far back as the Bible and find a similar conundrum. In Proverb 30:8, 9, the words of a prayer read, "Give me neither poverty nor riches; feed me with the food that is needful for me, lest I be full and deny you and say, 'Who is the Lord?' or lest I be poor and steal and profane the name of my God." And Proverbs 6:30, 31 reads, "People do not despise a thief if he steals to satisfy his appetite when he is hungry. But when he is caught he will repay seven-fold; he will give all the goods of his house." Granted, both verses are talking about burglary which is different from robbery. Burglary involves theft of property only while the robbery involves physically confronting another person with intimidation or the threat of harm in order to dispossess them of their belongings.

This is not to say that burglary is a victimless crime. For there is still personal loss and victimization. Not only that, but when goods are stolen from a store, it harms the community because shopkeepers tend to inflate their prices in order to cover the loss of potential thefts. The passage from proverbs shows the difference between burglary and robbery. There is pity for the thief who steals to secure his basic physiological needs, but it is also understood that what has been stolen can be replaced. However, with the physical confrontation of a robbery, what is stolen is not just property, but a person's psychological, emotional and possibly even physical well-being. These cannot be easily returned.

On "What We Do," Freeway expressed in his own way what Ice Cube had done thirteen years earlier on "Amerikkka's Most Wanted" when he rapped, "I think back when I was robbing my own kind, the police didn't pay it no mind." But Freeway helps to show that it is not just the police who pay no attention to the robbery of blacks. For Freeway and people "from the hood" that he knows "feel" him, robbing blacks at gunpoint is treated as if it were just as harmless and pitiable a crime as burglary or petty theft because the one who is being robbed is simply an expendable nigga. In his song, he goes as far as to admit that when he and his friends "F*ck niggas up" they "laugh about it."

This proves a second point. The expendable nigga not only struggles to secure his basic physiological needs, he also lives with a lack of safety because others may target him as a victim while pursuing their own needs. To draw attention to how important this issue of safety is, consider this: the culture of Hip Hop would likely have never been born had their not been a gang truce in the mid-1970s in New York City. The lack of safety with which individuals were living would have kept their creativity from manifesting or, at least, would have made it difficult to explore this creativity to the lengths which they eventually did. This might make it seem that Maslow was right about the pecking order of these "needs," i.e. first safety and then, later on and higher up, creativity. But it can also work in reverse. If individuals are encouraged to exist at the level of morality and creativity, with self-respect and respect for others, will they not have more of an incentive for working toward and keeping the peace which respects all life?

What's more, when gang activity exploded on the streets of California in the 80s, the lack of safety did not halt creativity. In fact, it gave creativity a target. Through Gangster Rap, youngsters simply used their art to secure their basic needs. They used their voices to cry out about their unsafe neighborhoods, putting the dual problems of gangs and police brutality in plain view. A rapper caught up in that scenario could also use his lyrics to bark threats at potential enemies. He could boast of owning or carrying guns in an effort to warn others to leave him alone. One could also rap about the various ways people in the neighborhood were meeting their basic needs, e.g. by committing crimes such as selling drugs. Struggling at these lower levels did not block or dull creativity.

Struggling at the lower levels also did not completely block morality. Much of the violence was bravado for the sake of self-defense, i.e., safety. And, surprisingly, the earliest Gangster Rappers did not claim to be drug-dealers. Many of them explicitly stated that they were not and spoke negatively about the enterprise. These rappers only claimed to be reporting on the activity of others who were selling drugs such as in N.W.A.'s 1988 song "Dope Man" where only Easy E. knew the life of a dealer. Today, however, many rappers actually claim to be the dope-man. Sadly, the subject matter of much of today's popular rap music consists of using and abusing expendable niggas (or their female counter-parts, discussed in chapter eight) in order to secure the first two levels of Maslow's hierarchy; the music hardly ever expresses life at the higher levels.

The Dependable Level

If one is able to make it past the level of safety, he can then bask in the blissful realm of intimacy. It is at the level of 'love and belonging' that the dependable nigga comes into play. This label is often reserved for individuals who help a person survive at the lower levels of 'physiological needs' and 'safety.' As the rapper Drake explains in DJ Khaled's song "No New Friends," he aims to "Stay down with his day one niggas." "Day one" refers to those individuals who were around the artist before he became famous; presumably, back when he "started from the bottom"; when he was struggling to eat, pay bills, or simply survive. It is the dependable nigga's job to assist in out-maneuvering expendables niggas and to help keep one safe from them. Once an individual has proven himself useful in this way, he is qualified to be "my nigga."

There is something positive in this designation. From one perspective, it can be said that human-beings spend their earliest years in life learning to differentiate between the self and the other: be it other people or things. Infants use their five senses to identify that which is a part of the self and that which is external. This is not an easy process as we have basic biological needs that are external to us but which must, somehow, become a part of us; such as food and water. On top of this, we grow bonds and attachments to the individuals who are responsible for helping us to meet these needs when we cannot provide them for ourselves, e.g. parents and siblings who feed us, clothe us and help to keep us safe.

The familiar faces of family members and friends help us to feel secure in an ever-changing and otherwise scary world. Psychologists will suggest that the well-adjusted person is the one who has properly differentiated between the self and the other but, who also, has developed healthy attachments to others – not too dependent upon them but not totally detached either.

Thus the designation of "dependable nigga" has both a positive and a negative aspect to it. Positively, it evinces an acknowledgement of the need for others. One cannot make it in this world, no less, up the rough side of the mountain, alone because people need people. Yet, negatively, with this designation, the one who is being depended upon is nonetheless, a nigga. He may be dependable to me, but to everyone else, he is still expendable. What this negative aspect fails to take into account is that, just like 'my nigga' may be seen as expendable to someone else, so also the individual who

I am willing to treat as expendable may very well be someone else's dependable nigga.

Hip Hop music, which reflects the way many young, black males think and operate, is full of this simultaneous regard and disregard for dependable and expendable niggas. In the song, "No New Friends" mentioned above, Drake sings, "F*ck all yall niggas, except my niggas." On C-Murder's 2000 album *Trapped in Crime*, the rapper was joined by West Coast legend Snoop Dogg for the song "Down for My Niggas." On the chorus they proclaimed "F*ck them other niggas cuz I'm down for my niggas." More than a decade later, in 2014 the rapper YG invited Young Jeezy and Rich Homie Quan to participate on the street anthem "My Nigga." The song is a serenade to his dependable niggas while at the same time it echoed C-Murder with the words, "I ride for my niggas, F*ck them other niggas." These songs, and this mindset, fail to realize that it is impossible to keep 'my niggas' safe while communicating to others that as long as a person is not 'your nigga,' it is okay to treat him or her as an expendable. This harkens back to the days of slavery when a black was worthless and expendable unless a white person saw value in him or her and was willing to claim the African as 'my nigger.' But even then, the slave was only valuable to its owner. To all else, he or she was expendable.

The Exceptional Level

Finally, we arrive at the top two levels of Maslow's hierarchy. Here is where the exceptional nigga begins to flourish. In the previous chapters we saw that Hip Hop music only began to include the concept of the exceptional nigga after the culture's art had become overpopulated with expendable ones. This is because it is impossible to have one without the other. Human nature will not allow for the acceptance of the self as expendable. Our instinct is toward self-preservation not towards perishing. If the neighborhood is full of expendable niggas, no one wants to believe that he or she is one of them. And yet, when working one's way up from the bottom of the hierarchy, struggling to survive, it seems the easiest way to rise is at the expense of others who are competing for the same resources as the self. The exceptional nigga must stand on the shoulders of dependable ones, who are standing on the backs of the expendable ones. Thus the pyramid is made.

As was previously mentioned in this chapter, when approaching the hierarchy from the bottom up, the soul or, ones sense of self (self-esteem, self-worth) is seen as the outcome of having achieved the lower levels. It flows from the success of surviving and climbing up the rough side of the mountain. When one listens to modern day, popular rap music, the truth of what has been said here is immediately evident. The high sense of self-esteem, of which many rappers boast in their lyrics, is directly tied to the lower levels of the hierarchical needs. Being able to wear high fashion, eat gourmet meals, drive and fly in luxury transportation, live in a nice home, have one's sexual 'needs' and desires met, to have the right people in one's circle, to feel safe or invincible – be it in the hood or in a court of law – all of these lower-level issues are presented as the reasons why an individual artist now has a sense of self-worth. It reveals that the developmental process of differentiation has not been successfully completed because one's sense of self cannot be well conceived without the use of all of these external things.

This materialist approach is the complete opposite of the metaphysical world-view which will be discussed in the next chapter. With the metaphysical, self-esteem is not the product of the lower levels but, rather, flows down from the higher level of actualization. This puts a different spin on the hierarchy which has implications for Hip Hop and the use of the 'N' word as well.

The Nigger in Charlotte's Web

Hip Hop culture did not invent the three uses of the 'N' word but modern, popular rappers demonstrate them perfectly well and encourage their ongoing use. If the danger of African Americans continuing to use the word in these ways has not been sufficiently laid out, perhaps it can be illustrated by a retelling of the classic children's fable – Charlotte's Web.

The story begins on Mr. Arable's farm. Fern Arable, the farmer's daughter, takes pity on a pig, a creature that was only meant to be sold or slaughtered. Before that time a pig's only worth was its market value. Pigs were fed well and allowed to grow big and fat, but not for their own sake, rather so that their owners could profit from them. Thus they were expendable. This would soon change though, not for all pigs, but for one special pig.

When Fern saw her father about to slaughter a small, weak piglet which seemed worthless to him, she could not help herself. She set her affections on the pig and begged for its life. She rescued and even named it, Wilbur. It was not wise to name a pig or to get too attached to one because, someday, the family would have to do to Wilbur what they did to all other pigs. But Fern continued to care for Wilbur. Through whatever emotional bond she had formed with him, she came to depend on Wilbur and he depended on her. Wilbur was 'her pig.'

After being transported to Fern's uncle's farm, the day finally came when the family was ready to take an ax to Wilbur. For even though Wilbur was Fern's pig, and thus special to her, he was not her father's pig, or her uncle's pig. To them, Wilbur was just as expendable as any other pig. At this point enters the wise and talented spider Charlotte. Charlotte had a great plan to make Wilbur more than just Fern's pig. Instead, she would show that Wilbur was exceptional. The spider began to spin and weave webs with words to spell out Wilbur's exceptional qualities. He was 'humble' and 'terrific.' This was not just any pig, rather, he was 'some pig.' Wilbur attracted so much attention that he was entered into the county fair where it became clear that he was too exceptional to be treated the same way as all other pigs. Thus, he was allowed to enjoy a long life back at the farm, surrounded by his many friends. The End.

If it is hard to see what this short story has to offer the present discussion, try this little experiment: Read the story again but this time, replace the word "pig" with the 'N' word and see if it does not come to life.

On the dis-record "Takeover," rap mogul Jay Z borrowed from an old adage when he rapped, "A wise man told me, 'don't argue with fools, cuz people from a distance can't tell who is who.'" This same principle can be said about the dangers of continuing to validate the 'N' word with all of its complexities. A particular African American might feel comfortable and confident in deciding which black people to call expendable, which dependable and which exceptional; but people at a distance, looking in from outside of the community cannot tell who is who. And since the historical default in America has been to lump all blacks into the expendable category until they can prove themselves otherwise (becoming a dependable friend or displaying just what it is that makes them exceptional), the use of the 'N' word only forces us to work over-time trying to identify which individuals are not expendable. But before we can succeed in doing this, the farmer's ax may fall, and with it, another black life.

Slim Jesus and Other Honorary Niggas

In 2015, an 18 year high school graduate from Hamilton, Ohio began his rap career under the name Slim Jesus. The rappers arrival on the Hip Hop seen caused quite a bit of dismay. Listeners struggled to understand the social significance of the artist's work as his frail physical frame struggled to support the weight of the claims made in his music. He rapped, "You ain't really about sh*t, stay out my spot, don't speak my name/ Or I'll pull up on your block at night, wearing all black and let that 40 (caliber gun) bang/ . . . I paid 350 for a Fendi belt and that double F hold up my strap/ A lot of yall just Twitter flex but this sh*t aint just a f*ckin' rap." The style of Hip Hop in which these lyrics were delivered is known as Drill rap. 'Drill' combines trap Hip Hop beats with the threat of violence and commitment to crime associated with the South-side of Chicago.

However, the confusion about Slim Jesus is not just that he seemed too small to pull off the capers communicated in his music. Rather, it was that Slim Jesus was white while the grit and grime of Drill music had, up until the time of his rise to fame, been by and about young black men in the streets of what has been dubbed 'Chi-raq.' In the first three months of its initial posting to YouTube, Slim Jesus "Drill Time" video reached over twelve-million views. While the typical Drill music video behavior (flashing money and pointing guns at the camera) was all present, what was absent was the customary Drill rap victim – Slim Jesus encountered zero "niggas," i.e. no strawmen on his hit song.

When asked about the absence of the word in his music in an interview with VLAD TV, Slim replied, "It's not that I feel like shouldn't or that I can't [say it], it's just a personal decision where I don't see why I would . . . I don't feel the desire to." When asked whether he thought white people should be allowed to say the word, the rapper responded, "I think white people sound corny saying that sh*t. But on like [whether] you can . . . f*ck it. It's a word." VLAD, who has interviewed everyone who is anyone in Hip Hop culture, counseled him, from one white male to another, "I don't say it either. . . That's been the best decision I've ever made."

Slim Jesus confessed that he was amazed to see that in the 'comments' section to his viral video, people had taken so much notice to the fact that his Drill rap has no 'N' words. But his amazement is astonishing to the sociologist. Aside from the artist's belief that whites in Hip Hop sound corny saying the word, there is a historical reason why they cannot use it at will. Blacks may refer to whites as 'my nigga.' And a white person, in very controlled environments, may be allowed to say the same to his black friends. But it is not permissible for whites to use the 'N' word as a strawman the way a black person might. The reason for this is not just based on the fact that whites once only meant to degrade blacks by use of the name.

The reason they cannot is because, even if whites are "niggas" is some sense, they are hardly ever, almost never, expendable niggas; at least not in the eyes of the institutions of America. Be they legal or political institutions, academic ones or places of employment, white people seem to always be seen as exceptional and to be more speedily embraced as dependable. Therefore, the ability to use "nigga" as a strawman is reserved for the people who know that at any given moment, because of the color of their skin, they can become one of those expendable bodies that have fallen and failed to make it up the rough side of the mountain. Thankfully, though, this is not the only way to approach Mount Maslow.

7

Navigating the Highs and Lows of Hierarchy (Part 2)

Suppose there was another way to approach Mt. Maslow. What if the rough road from the bottom to the top was not the only way to navigate the treacherous terrain? What if the terrain was, in fact, not so treacherous when traveling in the opposite direction, going from the top down? This is what a metaphysical worldview has to offer over and against the materialist view.

Metaphysical simply means 'beyond the physical or material world.' It is a way of looking at things which acknowledges truth beyond what is currently available to the human mind and the five senses of man. It asks questions about ultimate meaning, reality and origins. It is the child's incessant inquiry which asks 'where did

_____ come from?' and continues to ask this same probing question to each answer that is given. It sees the world, not as disintegrated matter which came to be in its current form only by chance; but as having something cohesive and grand as the cause and purpose behind it all. The search for this 'something' often leads to some kind of religious belief that sees mankind and the human soul not as a cumulative creation which evolves from the lower levels but, rather, as derivative and a microcosmic representation of something greater. In this view, having a soul, or strong sense of self, is not the outcome of achieving the lower levels. Achieving the lower levels are the outcome of having a soul.

Even before children are old enough to talk and to ask their curious questions, someone, some parent or guardian, is looking out for the child. Someone is giving the child the benefit of the doubt that he or she is valuable, creative, and morally inclined or, at least, designed to be. Because of this, the child's physiological needs, safety, and the need for love and belonging are provided. One thinks of the Hollywood adaptation of the book, *The Help*. The main character, a black maid serving a white family, is portrayed taking care of a little white girl. The maid is diligent in instilling a life-lesson into the child. She makes the little girl remember the words, "You is smart. You is kind. And you is important." The tragedy of the story is that this maid has spent so much time helping the white family that she has not had the time to invest in instilling this same lesson into her own offspring.

All parents want their children to be smart, kind and to have a sense of self-worth. But in communities where the 'N' word is frequently heard, something very different is instilled in children – low self-esteem and low expectations. Instead of acknowledging a child's higher hierarchical attributes and helping them to conceive of themselves in ways which draw on morality, creativity, and the ability to solve problems in ways that do not create more problems, the 'N' word demeans them by creating a blanket disclaimer to explain ignorant behavior. The phrase, "Niggas" is often breathed out to express the thought, 'What else can you expect from *certain* people.' On top of this, popular culture reinforces the myth that one's sense of self-worth will come, not from investing in the soul, but from the material things which we cannot live without.

The metaphysical view stands against this. At the top of Maslow's hierarchy, on the level of actualization, we find 'acceptance of the facts.' This refers to the ability to deal with reality as the rational mind perceives it to be. But for the metaphysically-minded, it is not acceptance of facts but, rather, the reception of truth; truth as revealed by some deity or, discovered by some clue found in the grand design of the universe. Embracing this truth is seen as the source of morality and creativity which leads to securing the lower hierarchical needs. Like many other ethnic groups, African Americans have a long history of using religion,

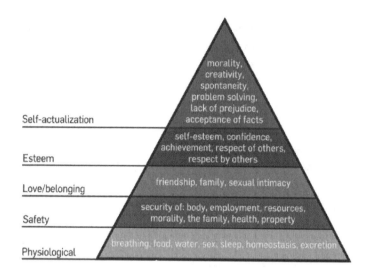

employing a metaphysical, top-down approach to combat the seemingly insurmountable challenges of climbing to the top. This history extends all the way up to the Conscious and Christian rap strands of modern day Hip Hop culture.

Does Religion Help?

Two of the world's most dominant religions, Christianity and Islam, have been helpful in giving African Americans a sense of self-worth in the face of unbridled racism and oppression. During the days of slavery, blacks in America found encouragement in the Christian faith which told of God rescuing the Children of Israel after 400 years of slavery in Egypt. The tales of God's power and will to deliver oppressed people resonated at the deepest levels of the souls of black folk.

But not only that; there was also the hope of life beyond the grave, free from the toils and sorrows of this life. A heaven where no more tears would fall and no one would be nearer to, or further from, the presence of God because of the color of one's skin; a heaven where there would be no "niggers" because God sent his son, Jesus, to die for white and black sinners alike, proving that he loved everyone the same – this was good news! One way or another, either by divine deliverance in this life or death followed by eternal paradise in the next, Christianity offered hope to the slave.

Having said this, it would be wrong to think that African peoples were only introduced to, and embraced Christianity, as a result of American slavery. This is far from the truth. For just after the time of Jesus, right as the first Christian church was forming in Antioch in the first century of the current Common Era, the Bible records that one of the earliest converts to the Christian faith was a high ranking Ethiopian official who served in the court of Candace, called Queen of the Ethiopians. And historians have shown that for the first 1000 years of its existence, Christianity was stronger in Asia and Africa than in Europe.[20]

Despite this, some African Americans have espoused the view that Islam is a more authentically African religion than is Christianity. This idea arose in the mid-20th century. It was the late 1950s when African Americans began to realize that many white, racist "Christians" remained unmoved by the plight of their black brothers and sisters in the faith. At the same time, other white Christians who were emotionally impacted by the Civil Rights Movement remained silent and would not speak out against injustice. Additionally, they advised black Christians to remain silent as well; to patiently and piously wait for the wheels of history to slowly turn in the favor of African Americans.

As a result of this frustration, in the early 1960s, the Nation of Islam, a Black Nationalist movement which originated in Detroit, Michigan in the 1930s, began to stand out as a militant alternative to the peaceful methods of the Civil Rights Movement. Malcolm X and other passionate, young, black leaders criticized the hypocrisy of the white church and the irony of the black church in embracing the religion which was used to enslave, segregate and oppress them. In the 1960s, many young African Americans began to break away from the black church in order to stand with the Nation of Islam. Black clergy could not offer their youth sufficient answers as to why their white, Christian brothers and sisters continued to refuse their cries for justice and equality. Did the Christian faith really give whites license to keep black people subdued, struggling to survive at the lower levels of the hierarchy of needs? And if so, what were blacks to do about it?

Throughout the 1960s there was growing debate within the black community over which methods were best suited to achieve the desired ends of the race – would it be peaceful protest or fighting fire with fire (or, perhaps, fire-arms)? What was unquestionable was that blacks would not live under white oppression and injustice. For the youth who were coming of age, influenced by the writings of Malcolm X; for those young adults who would soon initiate the Black Power Movement, fighting with fire seemed increasingly favorable. But this would only solve one side of the issue. The consciousness that the Black Power Movement promoted aimed to educate and graduate street niggas to the ranks of the historic bad nigga in order to fight for justice and equality, social reform and political empowerment. However, it was not just equality of treatment that mattered, but equality of being. Were black people subhuman in essence, or were they on the same level as whites?

There was another source which addressed this issue. This source took the idea of consciousness to a whole other level and dealt with, not just the black self as it relates to the outer world; but rather, the inner life of the soul in relation to the higher, metaphysical plane. Far from being niggers, this source taught that blacks were something else entirely. They were not simply equal with whites, blacks were much higher. And, even more than the Black Power Movement, this source played a major role in moorings of Hip Hop culture.

The 5% Nation of Gods and Earths

In 1964, one of Malcolm X's former students, known as Clarence 13X, branched off from the Nation of Islam to form the 5% Nation of Gods and Earths. One of

Clarence's chief objections to the sect he left was that Wallace Mohammad, the founder of the Nation of Islam, allowed himself to be worshipped as god. Instead, Clarence taught that it was not only the right of one man to claim that title, but that the black man, in general, was the personification of god on the earth. This divine identity, he taught, had been concealed from blacks by the devilish deeds of whites who knew but, for a time, have been able to supplant and subjugate the original black man.

Clarence developed a host of teachings, 120 lessons based on creative mathematical symbolism (Supreme Mathematics) which members were encouraged and expected to learn in order to gain full consciousness. Many people who have embraced Hip Hop over the years have no idea just how impactful this group has been on the culture. In his article on "The Muslim Roots of Hip Hop," author and visual artist Naeem Moheiamen argues that it is Islam which paved the way for Hip Hop, from the socially conscious, politically charged works of the Last Poets in the early 1970s to the 5% teachings of Clarence 13X which provided the metaphysical worldview for some of the most influential early, East Coast rappers in the game.

In a 2015 panel discussion, Conscious rapper, Talib Kweli admitted that as a teen, even he was a 5 Percenter, "for about two months," he laughed. But he surmised, "I don't even have the words to describe how much impact the 5 Percent Nation had on [early] Hip Hop artists. All of the biggest Hip Hop artists were 5 Percent rappers. In order to be the best you had to be 5 Percent. Rakim and [Big Daddy] Kane were 5 Percent rappers. You couldn't even consider yourself one of the best unless you could build with the god."[21]

Being able to "build with the god" might sound strange to uninitiated ears. The term 'build' is one of the many concepts gifted to Hip Hop culture from the Nation of Gods and Earths. It simply means to have constructive dialog, using the lessons of the Nation to advance one's knowledge of self. The other term, 'god' is the main point here. Of the many things the 5 Percent Nation did for early Hip Hop, teaching that the black man is the personification of god gave a sense of self-esteem and self-worth to young African Americans in New York City and made it unnecessary, and in many cases, impossible for the early leaders of Hip Hop culture to refer to themselves or other black men as "niggas." Moheiamen observed that in the popular urban greeting 'Sup G' [What's up, G], the 'G' originally stood for 'god' and not 'gangster' as was later the case when Hip Hop went west.[22] This is the main reason why East Coast rap was able to fight against embracing the 'N' word for several years even after Western and Southern Hip Hop had embraced it.

Christian Metaphysics

Talib Kweli spoke of "5 Percent rappers." However, none of the artists he referred to would have called themselves by that name when they were espousing the

Nation's views in their music. Much less would any of them have identified as 'Muslim rappers.' But this lack of labeling was not because individuals were embarrassed to have their art associated with their faith. On the contrary, it was because, for many during that time, the terms 'Muslim' and 'Hip Hop' could almost be seen as synonymous if you followed the trail. Consider this: early rap music thrived on its revolutionary traits; being revolutionary meant that one was following the trajectory of the Black Power movement; following that trajectory meant being conscious; consciousness, in the 1970s, came primarily through the Nation of Islam, the writings of Malcolm X, or the Nation of Gods and Earths; ergo being a Hip Hopper meant that one was, in some way, connected with or heavily influenced by the Muslim faith.

Because of the fluidity with which rappers moved between sects of Islam and other offshoots or variants of it, it was not always easy or important to narrow down just what one's proper religious designation was at any given time. In studying the ways in which sociology and faith have intersected in the lives of oppressed peoples, Mohaiemen argues that "Five Percent is in many ways a 'gateway' theology, which many African-Americans passed through to come in contact with other sects of Islam."[23]

Rappers in the 1970s and 80s did not have to call themselves 'Muslim rappers' because of the dominance of the faith's persuasion. For a good while, it helped keep the word "nigga" out of many mouths and elevated the musical conversation within rap above the first two levels of Maslow's Hierarchy. What would have helped with this elevation is if, along with Muslim rappers, there had been a host of Christian rappers in the culture as well. And, there most likely would have been, if only the black church had developed a more compelling response to the Black Power Movement and if the church, overall, did not have such a negative reaction to the rise of Hip Hop. In those days, even if a particular rapper had not gotten his consciousness through Islam, it was a foregone conclusion that whatever his or her metaphysical worldview (and there were several faiths being proclaimed in the inner-city in those days) it was almost certainly not acquired through Christianity.

Mohaiemon rightly points out that Islam's success in capturing the heart of the burgeoning Hip Hop movement was "aided by the black church's antagonistic relationship with Hip Hop." Even before the Gangster became a prominent figure in rap music, the black church closed its arms to the culture. Mohaiemon goes on to add that, "the Christians really hurt themselves by trying to demonize hip hop. Because they were attacking the most impoverished, and most socially, politically and economically denied people. So the youth heart hardened against the churches."

It was not that the church did not have a metaphysical, top-down approach to offer young African Americans who were looking for answers. It was more that, historically, American Christianity has been so pretentiously concerned with the higher levels of the hierarchy that it struggles to work itself out at the lower, basic levels of everyday life. Or, at least, that is the way it has been presented to black people. As the old saying goes, Christianity ran the risk of being 'so heavenly minded that it was of no earthly good.'

This was the case during slavery when the message whites preached to blacks was that all the comfort and relief they sought would come, not physically in this life, but only spiritually here; and then materially in the next life. These types of messages were used to keep slaves docile and complacent. But literate slaves found other passages of scripture in the Bible to encourage their flight or fight for freedom.

The case of the Presbyterian Church in America during the antebellum period is a fitting example of the impotency of historic, white Christianity as it relates to black life and self-worth. Clergymen from this cut of the cloth had been preaching and writing against the evils of slavery for at least eighty years before the Civil War. But "new school" Presbyterian ministers soon found themselves having to go outside of the Bible, relying more on common-sense realism and rationalism in order to refute "old school" members of their denomination. Northerners had no biblical response when leading southern, white ministers, such as James Thornwell argued that a literal interpretation of the Bible sanctioned American slavery. This argument silence many, not because it was convincing, but because for old school Presbyterian ministers, it was seen as more of a crime to not hold to a literal interpretation of Scripture than it was to not uphold the biblical commands of love and justice (at least as it related to Africans in America).

This only helped to weaken the Bible's influence on society since it was unable to speak powerfully and convincingly to the major moral issue of the day.[24] Yet it was not the Bible's inability to speak; but rather, white Christian's unwillingness to hear and apply the scriptures favorably on behalf of blacks. This unwillingness stemmed from the unaddressed issue of race. Slavery was one thing. But even after the institution was abolished by act of war, the issue of race was still lingering about. White Christians were part of the problem, even as they endeavored to be part of the solution. Before the war, in the North, leading Presbyterian theologian Charles Hodge maintained that if he had his way, blacks would be freed, but that also, they must remain disfranchised.[25] Thus throughout American history, good white Christians, even though they fought for freedom, very seldom led the way toward equality. These were two separate issues; one more realistic (and logical in the eyes of many) than the other.

Almost a century later, during the Civil Rights era, many whites wondered why Dr. King and his people were still marching and fighting. What was all this talk of equality, wasn't freedom enough? Many in the black church, looking at their white counterparts, were confused about what it meant to be a 'good Christian.' Should blacks suffer in silence while waiting on the Lord for equality and civil rights? Or should they press the injustices they endured onto the consciences of whites, using the Christian banner to champion their cause? Many older black Christians chose silence. Others stood with Dr. King. But in the mid-1960s, even King's voice was not loud enough, not angry enough for the youth of the growing Black Power movement. And so, the black church, perhaps, taking too much of its cue from the white church on the issues of the 70s, was out of touch with the revolutionary spirit of the age, and therefore, out of step with the Hip Hop generation.

Black Liberation Theology

Just like the Nation of Islam was a Black Nationalist spin on Islam proper, and the Nation of Gods and Earths was a spin-off of the Nation of Islam, geared to empower young blacks; so the Christian religion also experienced a theological experiment during 1960s and 70s, aimed at recapturing and empowering the hearts of black youth. But, just as was the case historically, this experiment was dismissed by white Christians for theological reasons, even while its sociological and humanitarian implications remained unaddressed.

James Cone is known as the father of Black Liberation Theology. In the late 1960s, as black clergy sought to provide an answer to the Black Power

Movement that would be consistent with their Christian faith, men like Cone began to realize that they did not have to look very far. For it seemed that African-Americans had always adapted the Christian faith to their socio-cultural circumstances.

Black Liberation Theology understands black Christianity as an "appropriation" of the religion that white slave masters gave to their slaves. It was blacks learning to talk about the issues of the soul in the only language that whites seemed to respect, the Bible. But unlike the 5 Percenters who claimed that the black man was god, Cone went the opposite direction and preached that God had become black. Cone was undaunted by conservative, evangelical critiques of his theology because it had become apparent that there was no use trying to find a common or universal theology, one that was held by both oppressors and the oppressed. Black theologians of the liberation stripe needed no longer seek white approval because the two groups had dissimilar aims and interests.

Having written his doctoral dissertation on Karl Barth, Cone analyzed his own definition of what it means for God to "be black" in light of Barth's theology. Cone was convinced that in a very real and theological way, at least during the Civil Rights era, God was black. For him, the true test of any theology was whether or not it allowed God to meet people in their experience. The key question for Liberation Theology is, 'where is there suffering in the world?' In the 1960s, the demonstrable answer for many black theologians was 'in the African-American community.' If that was the case, then that is where God was.

But it can be, and has been, stated even stronger than this. According to Cone, suffering tells us not just 'where God is'; it also tells us 'Who God is' because God identifies with the sufferer. Does the Bible support this idea? Cone draws an analogy here. In biblical history, God chose the Jews, an oppressed people, to be his own. He identified with them and liberated them so that they could participate in his liberating program for mankind. That was then. But now, "Black Power is the spirit of Christ himself; through it, blacks no longer hate themselves but recognize their worth; and whites are divested of their racism."[26]

Cone went on to explain that, "By choosing Israel, the oppressed people among the nations, God reveals that his concern is not for the strong but for the weak, not for the enslaver but for the slave, not for whites but for blacks."[27] And this has clear implications for the church. The church is not, he says, "Where the word is preached and sacraments rightly administered." Rather Christ is in the ghetto fighting the racism of churchly white people, not in peaceful, quiet suburban churches.[28] All Christians must become black, as long as blacks are the ones suffering. For that is what God does. In Jesus, "God became a despised Jew. But now, Christ is black, baby. Big lips and kinky hair. Christ is black because he is oppressed and oppressed because he is black."[29] Salvation, for Cone, equaled liberation (social, political, economic) and, says he, it always has.

This was an ingenious attempt to kill two birds with one theology. One the one hand, it aimed to sensitize evangelical Christians to the spiritual priority of empathizing with the black underclass. While at the same time, it could serve to show black youth that the Bible did, indeed, speak specifically to the current struggle of the black race. But it failed on both attempts. With conservative, evangelical Christians it failed because it made the once-for-all salvation event into something that was not uniquely significant in history but rather, something that was repeatable and found in every form of liberation occurring at any time in history. Thus, it was theologically unsatisfactory. On top of this, it incarnated and personified God in more ways than the Bible already had, and as 'black' no less. On the other account, Cone's theology failed with black youth because it included an element of suffering that seemed to call more for sympathy or empathy from others than for action from blacks. And action is what the Black Power Movement was all about.

Christian and Conscious Rap

As the Civil Rights era came to a close, the Nation of Islam remained vocal but Rap music became the leading voice, and Hip Hop the key identifier of the next generation. As for the black church, many of those who left it in the 1960s and 70s never returned.[30] Because of this, and the longevity of the church's unwelcoming stance on Hip Hop, the new voice of urban, black youth lacked any input from the church for almost the first 20 years of its existence.

The black Christian's absence from early Hip Hop culture is regrettable because it is likely that the presence of Christian rappers would have helped to add a much needed measure of accountability to the rap community. Not only that, but it could have safeguarded the culture against embracing the 'N' word as a suitable substitute for the average black man. The need for some kind of accountability became apparent in the late 80s and early 90s as quite a few inconsistencies began to arise from rap camps populated by Muslims rappers, be they 5 Percenters, Nation of Islam or Sunni. Hip Hop seemed to have a strange and, at times, unhealthy impact on the practice of the Muslim faith, especially amongst 5 Percenters. As activist and educator Asida Banjoko points out:

> No other Islamic sect in the world accepts drinking alcohol. Yet Brand Nubian are known to smoke weed by the pound and drink like fish. Poor Righteous Teachers seem to be the only group from the 5 Percent that shuns drugs, alcohol and foul lifestyles. All the talk about spaceships doesn't help either. The 5 Percent Nation really hurt al-Islam because of their inability to hold on to any theological concept consistently; not to mention their violence and misogyny, which hurts all true believers.[31]

The rap groups mentioned by Banjoko are just a few of the many names that can be mentioned in this regard. However, when Christian rap finally began to pick up traction on the East Coast in the late 1990s, one of its chief aims was challenging 5 Percent rappers at both ends of the hierarchy: on the nature and identity of God and man on one end; and on living a consistently righteous life when it came to pursuing physiological needs, safety and the need for intimacy on the other end. Rap groups like The Cross Movement, of which the present author was a member, Corey Red & Precise, and Todd Bangz were instrumental in this history. Not only did Christian rappers list the vices mentioned by Banjoko as struggles to be overcome, as in The Cross Movement's "Creature Double Feature," they also projected and promoted a consistently positive image of black, urban males.

Because of a commitment to the belief that man is made in the image of God, Christian rap has never embraced the word "nigger" as an appropriate designation for oneself, one's friends or one's enemy. In fact, any time the word is used within the culture's art, there is blowback. On his 2013 album *Talented 10th*, Christian rap affiliate Sho Baraka gave social commentary when he stated, "I guess I'm stuck here on Nigga Island/ Where niggas be wildin'." The debate it sparked in the Christian Hip Hop community further fueled Sho Baraka's decision to cease being labeled as a Christian rapper and to be only affiliated with the genre. Conscious rapper KRS One once remarked that he did not think Christian rap could be viable for this very reason. KRS was under the impression that Christians were unable to speak the way real Hip Hoppers spoke.

They were not, he thought, allowed to say things like, 'Yo' and 'Wassup Homeboy,' etc. Even though 'The Teacher' was mistaken on this point, the backlash over Sho Baraka's "nigga" lyric does show the difference in cultural norms practiced by Christian and non-Christian rappers.

If all of the metaphysical forces that aided African Americans during the most tumultuous years of the struggle for freedom and equality would have been present from the beginning of the new culture, Hip Hop as a movement, following the Civil Rights Movement, would have been immensely helped. Today, as those who were born in the 1970s and 80s are entering their 30s and 40s, urban Christians within that age-range are helping the church reach out to the culture it once shunned in order to pour in its spiritual nutrients.

Through Christian rappers, the church now gets to say that it has embraced Hip Hop culture. Though in many churches, aspects of the culture are enjoyed only on 'Youth Sunday' (typically the 5th Sunday of the month, a phenomenon that occurs only several times a year). This is the least that can be done. But if Christian rap is treated like a stepchild in the church; it is treated like a foster-child outside of it. For even though the church, to some degree, has embraced Hip Hop, still, Hip Hop culture does not always immediately embrace Christian rappers. This is not simply because of the surface reason that is often given, i.e. that Christian rap is corny. By now, thanks to the groundbreaking work of

Cross Movement Records artists and the more recent, award winning work of Reach Records artists, there has certainly been enough data to dispute the 'corny' claim.

But what has made Christian rap stand out as an oddity in the Hip Hop community is its lack of the two major influences which helped to steer the culture in the days of its formation: Black Power and Blaxploitation. As for the lack of Black Power, Christian rap can sometimes come across as color-blind because it does not acknowledge blacks as niggas; not in the ironic sense or in any other. Also, it does not often draw attention to the affliction of blacks, the misdeeds of whites or the racially prejudiced systems of control at work in society. Instead, it has tended to focus more on the sins of humanity in general and the need for salvation.

When Christian rappers do specifically target bad behavior, a popular topic tends to be 'drug dealers on the block.' Even though East and West coast, Conscious and Gangster Rappers used to condemn drug dealing as well, Hip Hop reached a point in the late 80s when the criminal became the celebrated figure. The lack of jobs in the inner-city, the introduction of crack-cocaine into the drug market and the increased antagonism of police made the content of 1970s Blaxplotation films seem like a possible escape route; a fictional one for some and a factual one for others. But the Christian rapper's commitment to biblical ethics will not allow him to make such moral exemptions for the hood's heroes.

Hence, Christians in Hip Hop do not appear to be 'down with the struggle' for survival when they speak out against the black criminal's immoral actions while trying to secure the lower levels of the hierarchy.

Islam's rappers are not immune to this kind of pushback as modern, popular Hip Hop tends to lean away from Black Power and swing more in the direction of Blaxploitation. In 2015, two legendary battle-rappers, Murda Mook and 5 Percenter, rap veteran Loaded Lux, faced off for the second time in what was destined to be an epic showdown. But things went downhill very quickly for Lux when his opponent challenged him on two related fronts: first for committing to a metaphysical worldview that would not allow him to support the struggle of inner-city, black criminals; then, second, for contradicting himself by breaking out of his Black Power "box" in order to, lyrically, treat some blacks as expendable.

In the past, Lux had used his raps to preach against dealing drugs and other self-destructive and community crippling behaviors. Mook had this in mind when he rapped. "Nigga shut ya lips/ You think we f*ckin with that righteous bullsh*t/ when nigga's mothers was out here struggling?" Mook then turned to chastise the crowd as he completed the line. In light of the hardships being experienced in the ghetto he asked those in attendance, how could "yall let him dis niggas for hustlin?" Later, in the same round, Mook picked up the theme and charged, "It was you who dissed us for selling drugs and toting glocks . . . you put yourself in a box/ cause now if [you] ever try to rap hard . . . it's still against what [you] believe in/ [you'll] be depicted as a fraud."

The dagger was thrust into Loaded Lux's musical metaphysics in the second round when Mook called him out on the contradiction contained. He rapped, "Word around Harlem [is you] joined the Nation of Radical Israelites . . . and you supposed to promote the struggle, the fight, but something ain't right/ In your raps you be pumpin all this Black Power sh*t/ but then every other word is "Nigga" coming out your lips/ that's preposterous/ you are more hypo-critical than a dying hippopotamus/ . . . you fake-ass 5 Percenter."

This is ironic. As long as being 'down for the struggle' is used to justify being bad for no good reason, the unrighteous bad nigga will have the power to shame those who advocate righteousness. And as long as those who advocate righteousness walk in contradiction, claiming to be about helping uplift black people while at the same time, addressing their fellow man as "nigga," they will not be able to answer those who question their commitment as Murda Mook did Loaded Lux.

But those who operate with a metaphysical worldview – and who are consistent in their orthodoxy and orthopraxy – prove that they are more than down for the struggle; they are up it. Their top-down approach keeps their morality and creativity tied together and guides the way they pursue the lower hierarchical needs. Where it is more a community of faith and accountability, Hip Hop culture has the means and motivation to pick up where the Civil Rights movement left off in imparting values to the next generation, instilling a sense of self-worth that does not rely on materialism. These communities must be created and cultivated in the midst of the broader culture in order to create a counter-culture. In this counter-cultural space the word "nigga" is just as offensive on black lips as it is on white lips. And there is constant affirmation that African Americans can be dependable and exceptional without having to be someone's nigga. The things that popular, modern rappers teach young blacks to rely on in order to gain self-esteem do not matter to the metaphysically minded, for their sense of self-worth comes from above, not from below.

In the latter years of Abraham Maslow's life, the psychologist amended his pyramid. After looking back at his own life and efforts at self-actualization, Maslow found the need to add another level at the top of his hierarchy – Self-transcendence. This, he said, only comes from acts altruism and spirituality as one seeks to give the self over to that which is higher than the self and act on behalf of others. True as this may be, the metaphysically-minded would say that this stage would not have taken so long for Maslow to reach if he would had begun with spirituality. By starting at the top, not only does one acknowledge his own soul and self-worth, but also the worth of others who, in no way, deserve to be oppressed at the bottom and left struggling to survive. When people are viewed this way, no one is expendable.

In summary, the word "nigger" is at best a celebration of those who have made it to the top and become exceptional at the expense of others and, at worst a label used to justify treating other human beings as expendable. It is both of these at once since it is impossible to have one without the other. In between these two polar ends there is the dependable nigga and gradations of the expendable nigga. All of these ideas should be rejected along with the word which carries them. The assumption that anyone is qualified to rename another person in this way is both an overestimation of the self and an underestimation of others. This should be challenged as often as the word is heard until the word "nigger" becomes as offensive on black lips as it currently is upon the lips of whites.

In 2015, the newest attempt to salvage the word was put forth by rapper Kendrick Lamar. At the end of his *To Pimp a Butterfly* album, Kendrick educated his listeners on an Ethiopian word meaning 'king' or 'royalty.' The word is 'Negus.' According to him, this is what African Americans should mean to convey when they use the word with one another. Kendrick is not only attempting to salvage a word, but rather a people who have been verbally abused by the word "nigger" which he believes to be a cognate of 'negus.' But if history can teach us anything here, it will be that valiant efforts to redefine the word will not win out over the negative connotations of the past which are waiting to attach themselves to each current usage. If it is allowed to live on, the next generation will marvel at how long the word has been able to survive and yet, how poorly the self-esteem, self-respect, and sense of community among those who are named by it struggle to exist at all.

Appendix

Navigating the 'B' Word

"Niggas take off your coats, ladies act like gems," are the instructions from A Tribe Calles Quest member Q-tip on the 1993 song "Award Tour." As yet another group embraced the 'N' word, comfort could at least be taken in the fact that women were still being respected as "ladies" by some members of the Hip Hop community. This was a refreshing lyric at the time, particularly because, as rap music became oversaturated with the 'N' word, it seemed that, correspondingly, black women were being downgraded in status as well. With increasing frequency, the 'B' word was used to refer to the object of a rapper's affection or aggression.

Even before N.W.A. ushered the 'N' word into Hip Hop's musical vocabulary, rappers were making occasional references to women as "bitches." In 1987, Oakland, California rapper Too $hort expressed himself as a pimp and talked about his experiences with women on the album *Born to Mack*. It was obvious that the rapper believed he was dealing with a particular kind of female whom society would not mind him labeling a bitch. In 1989, he returned with the album *Life is Too $hort* and continued his trend of renaming women with degrading terminology.

Seemingly aware of his verbal violations on the album, the rapper invited a female rap duo named Danger Zone to join him on the song "Don't Fight the Feeling." The original purpose of the girl-group was to provide an artistic portrayal of younger women refusing the rapper's sexual advances. But the group took it a step further and proceeded to lyrically dis Too $hort on behalf of all women for the way he constantly referred to them as bitches, hoes and sexual objects. Though Too $hort rewrote his two verses in order to "get them back" and even went as far as to invite another male rapper on the song to dis the young women for him, he refused to remove or change Danger Zone's lyrics, even when other people in his circle teased him for letting the young girls get the best of him in the musical back-and-forth.

In 2012, after recording over twenty rap albums, Too $hort looked back at his career and listed his 25

Most Essential Songs. He ranked "Don't Fight the Feeling" at number twenty and recalled why it was important for him to leave the girls' verses on the song unmolested. The legendary rapper explained, "It's like, you talk all this sh*t about girls, how come they can't talk sh*t back? It's an unfair environment, you know?"[32] Too $hort was not alone in his desire to create a more fair environment for women to "talk back" in Hip Hop. In 1990, Ice Cube invited female rapper Yo-Yo to collaborate on the song "It's a Man's World." Aside from challenging Ice Cube's superiority and calling him out for alleged sexual inadequacies, Yo-Yo added that it might be a man's world "but it wouldn't be a damn thing without a woman's touch." Through efforts like these, male rappers attempted to atone for their sexist sins.

On the East Coast, in 1987, Public Enemy had used the 'B' word to refer to the same type of woman as Too $hort. On the album, *Yo, Bum Rush the Show*, lead rapper Chuck D talked about a female who thought she was "so sophisticated," but who was in fact a "Sophisticated Bitch" who turned her nose up at dark-skinned men but sold her body to a different, brighter-skinned clientele for money and drugs. In 1988, in the first installment of EPMD's "Jane" saga, rapper Parish Smith wanted to be alone with a lady love-interest but the woman had brought along a friend. And so, he asked his partner Erick Sermon to help him out and "Chill with the bitch" Jane while he and his lover went elsewhere to become intimate.

These were still the early years. Rappers were just then becoming comfortable with using the 'N' word in Hip Hop art. Similarly, the 'B' word was rare, but not unheard of. Its vocalization in this genre was likely a reflection of how it was being used in real life. Originally, in the urban arena, the 'B' word was reserved for women who had brought reproach upon themselves, usually by being sexually active in a way men did not approve of or, the reverse; by refusing the sexual advances of an interested male. The rap group N.W.A. describe a regular occurrence in the 'hood' on their 1988 song, "Gangsta, Gangsta." With six "niggas" in a car, they ride past a young female who is walking alone and minding her own business. After propositioning her and getting no favorable response, Ice Cube raps, "She was scared and it was showin'/ we all said 'F*ck you bitch' and kept going."

It is not just when women exercise control over their own sexual lives that they are likely to be labeled with the 'B' word, but women in the business world have often complained that they are seen as bossy or as bitches whenever they do things that, typically, a man would be praised for doing, e.g. speaking up for oneself, demanding that a job be done a certain way, or not acquiescing to the demands of others.

No matter what women do, they have not been able to get away from this nasty name. And so, as was the case with the word "nigga," rather than fighting against it, at some point in the 1990s, young women began to embrace being "bitches" and tried, somehow, to change its meaning into a positive one. It should not be forgotten, however, that before the word began to grow in popularity in broader American culture, it was first used within Hip Hop culture, and there was no positive side to it until both male and female rappers began to apply it in new ways. As a result of these cultural shifts, the word functions much like and plays by many of the same rules as the 'N' word. Just a few of the principles that have been applied to the word "nigga" will be applied to the word "bitch" in order to demonstrate the dangers cultures face when their dialect is detached from their values.

Bitches are Niggas Too

When the 'B' word is used against women, it is often because a female is acting in an aggressive or assertive manner, the way men expect other men to behave. However, when the 'B' word is used to refer to men, it is usually because a man is acting in a passive or sensitive manner, the way men typically expect women to behave. For instance, on the 1991 album *Original Gangster*, in the song "Bitches 2" rapper Ice T explains to women why they should not be offended when he uses the 'B' word to refer to them. His reasoning is simple: because some niggas are bitches too. He then describes scenarios where men display dishonorable character traits and are, therefore, worthy of being called what women generally are in his mind, bitches. This was supposed to make women feel better about the terminology. But it did not immediately shift the culture in that direction.

Two years later, in 1993, Queen Latifah, responded to every black man who would dare use that wretched word to refer to a black woman. In the song "Unity" she forcefully and rhetorically rapped, "Who you callin' a bitch?" In the chorus, Latifah encouraged other women by telling them "you're not a bitch or a hoe." The "Ladies First" rapper was right to reject the term. But she seemed to only dispute certain aspects of its application while leaving the door open for other possible ways it could be used. Like the 'N' word, "bitch" has a semantic range that allows for more than one possible meaning. To be specific, it carries the expendable, dependable and exceptional ideas, just as well. And it impacts the culture just as severely.

Expendable Bitches

Unlike the case of the "expendable nigga," when men speak about females as "bitches" in the expendable sense, they do not mean to convey that a woman's actual life can be taken without giving it a second thought. Instead, they mean that she no longer has a place in a man's life one he has gotten what he wants from her. As Ice Cubes states in the song, "It's a Man's World," "after I do ya, I never knew ya." In inner-city slang, the phrase "catching bodies" (which is usually used to refer to committing homicides) is used by males to speak of having an increasing number of sexual exploits with women. "Bitches" are, in this sense, expendable once they have met a man's sexual needs. This is the aspect of the term that was rejected by Hip Hop's first Queen.

As strong a stance as she took for her gender, Latifah left the door slightly ajar to receive disrespect from her male peers. Speaking of the 'B' word on the song "Unity" she says, "There's an exception to the rule. I don't be gettin' mad when we playin' it's cool." She then warns, "But don't you be callin' me out my name." Like the 'N' word, there is room between friends to use it playfully. It is thought that the strength of the relationship removes the harm which would, otherwise, be present in the term. And, yet, when a woman allows a man to joke with her this way, inevitably, there comes a day when she is not sure if he is joking or being serious. Because he has gotten used to calling her "out of her name," or, to put it in the language of this book's first chapter, because he has been renaming her for so long, he has been conditioning her throughout their relationship so that she gradually allows herself to be treated in a way that corresponds to the name she has accepted. She has likely overlooked small ways in which this has been happening until, one day, she suddenly, and often painfully, is made aware that she is being disrespected.

Hip Hop did not begin the trend of black men using black women to serve and satisfy their own desire for pleasure or need for a boost in self-esteem. In fact, it is a mistake to see these two motivations as separate driving forces. For black men, the need for higher self-esteem has been tied to sexual activity since the days of Reconstruction in the years after slavery. The father of Black Liberation Theology, James Cone, wrote about this cultural phenomenon as it relates to African American men who sang and popularized Blues music in the first half of the twentieth century. For those artists, talking overtly about ones sexuality was a way to affirm that "I am a M-A-N," in a world of white supremacy that denied humanity to African Americans and treated men like boys.[33] This helped black men to feel affirmed in their manhood but the negative side-effect was that it reduced black women to being mere sexual objects. Recall the discussion concerning approaching Maslow's Hierarchy from the bottom up (in chapter six). When people are oppressed and made to feel powerless, often they turn to oppressing others in an attempt to regain a sense of mastery over their own lives. They do not always immediately realize that they have substituted 'mastering others' for 'controlling their own fate.'

It is difficult for ladies to "act like gems" when "niggas" take off their coats and proceed to treat women like bitches. In the early 1990s, Queen Latifah, along with fellow "femcee" (female emcee) Monie Love were a part of a rap collective known as the Native Tongues. These jazz-influenced, Hip Hoppers were known for introducing "Afro-centricity" into the culture during that time. One of the collective's most popular songs, "Buddy" featured Monie Love along with the Jungle Brothers, De La Soul and Q-tip from a Tribe Called

Quest. The song was a playful celebration of casual sex as well as a musical Public Service Announcement about safe-sex. The light-hearted nature of the production, along with Monie Love's gleeful participation, made it easy to miss the fact that this ode to sexuality-without-fidelity was the very ethic that lay at the base of Queen Latifah's objection in her "Unity" song. Even though her Native Tongue brothers were not calling women "bitches," they were still treating them as expendable objects to be used for men's gratification and to boost their self-esteem.

This is why concerned Muslims monitoring the culture, such as Asida Banjoko (see chapter 7), had a problem with supposed conscious rappers, especially those who claimed to be Muslim or 5 Percent. Take for instance the group Brand Nubian who, on their 1993 album *In God We Trust* rapped, "I'll steal your hoe when I'm on the microphone doing my show." This was the chorus to the song "Steal Ya Ho" which antagonized listeners by boasting of the sexual exploits that Brand Nubian group members, all of whom were 5 Percenters, had planned with another man's "hoe."

It is not a coincidence that rappers talking about what they will do with "your girl," or "your hoe" or "your bitch" only became popular after "niggas" had become the strawmen of Hip Hop. The roots of this go all the way back to slavery when black men in America were emasculated by having to watch the women they loved be taken from them and raped as well as having to watch their families be torn apart without being able to protect them. Historically, this is how you treat a black man who is a nigga. But if you mistreat the black man you must mistreat the woman who is attached to him—the two go hand in hand. This is why it is almost a guarantee that on any rap album where the artist boasts of injuring expendable niggas, he will also brag about how intimate he is able to become with an expendable nigga's "bitch."

In 2011, rapper J. Cole, who has always flirted with Conscious Rap, displayed just a modicum of remorse for the way he has endorsed this type of boasting. On the song "How High" he rapped:

[I'm] so sick that I could f*ck your bitch

Nigga please, my squad stack plenty of G's

And if your girl like to smoke we got plenty of trees

As the problems of the world unfurl

My niggas hit the trees like squirrels

Tryna get a nut with ya girl

[I] think I need to quit tryin'

[Be]fore some nigga out there try to hit mine

Karma for the Karma Sutra

Aside from the 'what goes around comes around' effect of Karma, J. Cole could have gone further to ask, 'even if what goes around doesn't come back around to me, why am I okay with doing something like this to someone else?' The answer would be startling: 'because the one I am doing this to is just a nigga. And the female I am using as a prop to belittle this nigga is just *his* bitch. The nigga that I am doing this to may depend upon her, but to me, she is expendable.' Spelling it out this way reveals the problem: uplifting the black race means fighting for the honor of every man and every women as well as the black family. But misogynistic lyrics lift a community's men-folk above its women and, when these lyrics are celebrated and lived out, they tear families apart.

Dependable and Exceptional Bitches

In the new millennium, rapper Nicki Minaj adopted the practice of referring to her devoted fans as "My bad B*tches." Being a "bad bitch" helped women to feel good about embracing the title since it seemed as if they would not be able to escape it. Much like the 'N' word, many females opted to own the title and give it a new meaning. If being "bossy," handling one's business and standing up for oneself sexually and professionally was a bad thing for women to do; and if, in the eyes of men this made them "bitches," then women, in growing numbers, began to take pride in being "Bad Bitches." Furthermore, if no man would claim them because of their "badness," then these women would claim one another. For many, the term "my bitches" functions much the same way as the phrase "my niggas" does for black men.

However, in order to qualify as such, one cannot be what is considered a "basic bitch." This is the term that is used to speak of a female who allows herself to be viewed and used as expendable. In an interview with

Vlad T.V., Nicki Minaj denied that she advocated promiscuous sex in her music, stating that, instead she only promoted "sex appeal." She went on to warn women that "If every nigga can say that he had it" (referring to sexual intercourse with a particular female) "then you're not a bad bitch; you're not on my team anymore."[34] In this way, Nicki believes that she is empowering women.

As is the case with the 'N' word, the 'B' word is also used by women to shame their peers out of engaging in behaviors that reflect poorly upon all women. "Bad bitches don't do what these basic bitches do," it is said. Interestingly, though, just like with the expendable nigga, it is not just a matter of shaming others. Rather, labeling other women as "basic" is often an opportunity to boost the self-esteem of women who desire to be seen as exceptional. "These basic bitches *can't* do what us bad bitches do." Thus, another strawman argument is built. By verbally attacking and tearing down anonymous "basic bitches," a woman can draw attention to her own exceptional qualities. So even though women may seek to empower themselves by appropriating the 'B' word, it has actually worked to divide them and weaken their cause. And, just like with the acceptance and continued use of the 'N' word, people looking from a distance can't tell the difference between the expendable and the exceptional, the "basic" and the "bad" bitch. In the end, they are all likely to be treated the same.

It's a Man's World

If it is true that hurt people hurt people, it is also true that oppressed people oppress people. Hip Hop's femcees did not begin calling themselves and other women "bitches" suddenly and from out of the blue. Nicki Minaj is only the latest in a long line of females who have grown tired of being subjugated by men, and in turn, have begun persecuting other women in order to regain some sense of power. In 2000, Florida rapper Trina released her debut album *Da Baddest Bitch*. Trina was introduced to the world by the rapper Trick Daddy. From the name alone, one can see the influence of the Blaxploitation era. Trick Daddy is clearly a reference to one of the world's oldest professions, i.e. pimping. Trina's album, *Da Baddest Bitch*, when combined with Trick Daddy's name, calls to mind one of the world's other oldest professions, prostitution. What is a pimp without "bitches?", and what good is there in being just a basic bitch? The artist took pride in being "the baddest one" i.e. the one who could bring in the most money for her pimp.

On the title track to the album, Trina rapped, "Get them niggas for all you can," and encouraged women to use their sexuality to get money from men. In the second verse, she warns men that if they are broke, sex is out of the question. The artist takes a great degree of pride in having reversed certain roles and expectations with her male clientele. She will not perform particular sexual acts upon them, but they must perform them for her.

After she has used a man, she is on to the next one. She explains, "You can never be my only one, cuz I want too much sh*t, want too much done." The concept of the song is to show what a "bad bitch" does. She uses men the way men have used women. She has taken control of her sexuality. She asks, in the second verse, "Where my bad bitches at?" And they reply, "Right here!" All of this promotes the idea that women have had to be "bad" in order to be exceptional and survive in a male dominated world. And only bad bitches are dependable bitches.

Like N.W.A. yelling "F*ck the police," Trina signs off every chorus of her song with harsh words for her oppressors. However, it is not the law with whom she takes issue. Instead she raps, "I'm getting paid yellin' 'F*ck a man.'" If women like Trina are "bitches," bad, basic or somewhere between, men bear the responsibility for producing that quality. It was the oppressive attitudes and actions of men, along with double standards as it relates to marital infidelity, which led to the Woman's Liberation Movement and Free-Love experiments of the twentieth century. Many credit these events as marking a drastic change in American morality and beginning the breaking down of family life throughout the country. But, for better or worse, women were simply desiring to play by the same social rules as men. Interestingly, though, in the case of Hip Hop, men actually asked women to become "bad bitches." This is how they seduced females into embracing the new name.

In 1993, West Coast legend Snoop Dogg rapped "To all my niggas, and my bitches, put your mother-f*ckin' hands in the air." The "Dog-father" as he has dubbed himself, had full confidence that his musical commands would be obeyed. How was he so sure? Women, at that time, were not yet used to responding positively to the negative name, especially when elsewhere, Snoop rapped, "Bitches ain't sh*t but hoes and tricks." But, the rappers commands were easy to receive because of the addition of the possessive term "my." This changed the tone of the offensive language in the song. These were not just niggas and bitches being told to put their hands in the air, but "my niggas" and "my bitches." In the same year, Hip Hop artist Apache rapped, "I need a Gangsta Bitch." The video depicted young women, dressed in baggy clothes and bandanas pulling out guns on other females and robbing them of their possessions. Apache saw himself as a bad nigga and correspondingly needed a bad bitch. The more bad, the more dependable she would be. But she was also expendable. At the end of the song, he reveals that his lady love was so illegal that she has been sentenced to prison. He shrugs off the loss and asks, "so who will be my next Gangster Bitch?"

Just three years later, in 1996, the world was introduced to Lil Kim and Foxy Brown. Like others in the Hip Hop community, the name 'Foxy Brown' is a throwback to the Blaxploitation era, specifically the film of the same name starring Pam Grier. What made Kim and Foxy stand out was not just the fact that the identified themselves as "bad bitches," but that they believed they were "bad meaning good." The "good" came from two directions: one, because they were able to boast of their financial independence and two, because they were dependable in the eyes of their male counterparts. Yet, they were clearly still very dependent on the approval of the "bad niggas" who had requested the presence of a Gansta Bitch. Over a decade after her entrance into the rap world, Lil Kim rapped about her exceptional qualities, explaining that she was the "Queen Bitch, supreme bitch, kill a nigga for my nigga by any means bitch."

In 1999, just before Trina released *Da Baddest Bitch*, East Coast rap trio The Lox, along with the Ruff Ryders, were climbing up the charts with one of their most successful songs which advertised, "I need a Ride or Die Bitch." Philadelphia female rapper and actress, Eve accompanied the group on the track and co-signed the concept that only a criminally bad bitch is exceptional enough to satisfy a bad nigga.

These examples might be viewed as simply entertainment and just artistic expressions, but art is a cultural exploration of the question, 'what's worth reproducing?' There may indeed be something worth reproducing in these cultural artifacts. But to incorrectly identify what that is only compounds the social pathology in the neighborhoods where the word of these songs are lived out. The desire for love and belonging, for intimacy, or self-esteem and spiritual transcendence, all of these are admirable. If however, morality is removed from ones attempt to acquire these things, and if these attempts are portrayed as worth reproducing despite their negative repercussions, then the question must be asked, "Is this art serving or doing a disservice to the culture for which it was created?"

B's in the Trap

In 2012, Nicki Minaj released the hit single, "Beez in the Trap." This was 'Ebonics' (ebony-phonics) for "I am always located in the trap." To break it further down, "trap" is slang for "streets" or the place where the game (drug-game) is played and dealers live with the risk of being caught by police and locked in jail. However, even apart from this, women like Nicki are caught in a different type of trap. It is the same one that applies to those who self-identify as "niggas." The same rules of ascendancy concerning Maslow's Hierarchy of Needs can be applied to the 'B' word and the 'N' word. Going from the bottom to the top is still the worst way to approach the hierarchy. Sadly, some are led to believe that this is how they must live their lives. Those who are looked at as "basic" or "expendable bitches" are identified as existing at the two lowest levels. As we have already seen, when starting at the very bottom, morality is not yet a factor. Thus, a woman can, and must do, whatever is necessary to survive here. She can be used or use her body in any way in order to meet her needs. Notice, that Maslow has placed "sex" at the level of physiological needs, and yet, has placed intimacy,

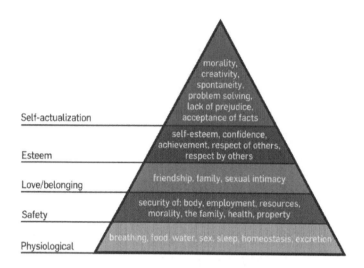

love and belonging at another, higher stage. Thus, when going from the bottom to the top, "bitches" are sexually expendable and should not expect to find or even be concerned with fidelity. This sheds more light on Nicki Minaj's comment concerning what it takes to be one of her "bad bitches" and why some women cannot attain this status. If safety, love and intimacy do not become concerns until after the lower physiological needs are met, it actually makes sense that so many "basic bitches" are willing to do sexually unsafe acts in order to feel fulfilled at the most base level of the hierarchy.

However, these women do not have to remain basic. If they can prove their reliability, they might eventually rise to the level of being "dependable bitches." Once they achieve this, they will get to experience a sense of belonging and true intimacy. Bear in mind, however, that often, becoming someone's "dependable bitch" also means being a "bad bitch." Meeting this requirement is risky because it is up to each woman to determine if "bad" means "bad" or if "bad" means "good" in each of the relationships she desires to maintain. In his 2012 song "Bitch Bad," conscious rapper Lupe Fiasco detailed the confusing dilemma young men and women face when they grow up with different understandings of what it means for a woman to be a "bad bitch." Does it mean that she handles legitimate business with just as much professional ambition as any man? Or does it mean, like Trina raps, that she uses her sexuality to "get them niggas for all she can?"

Either way, whenever a woman accepts the 'B' word as a proper designation, self-esteem will not be true "self-esteem." Rather it will be based on the respect received from others who might be impressed by the way she secures her lower hierarchical needs. Just as with the acceptance of the 'N' word, if she cannot secure the lower needs, she will lack self-esteem and fail to achieve the higher levels of actualization and transcendence.

What is the solution to this? As seen in chapter seven, approaching life from the opposite direction is the best answer. Rather than acknowledging and tending to the human soul after the long, arduous process of climbing Mount Maslow, it is best to begin at the top. Acknowledge the grander realities of our shared experience. Ask the deeper questions about our existence and meaning and attempt to understand the flow of history and the significance of the present moment.

Asking these questions only begins the process. Next comes evaluation of the answers and then the application of whatever is accepted as truth. For Hip Hop culture, in particular, one wonders what it would have been like if there had been more than just a handful of Queen Latifah(s) and Lauryn Hill(s), women who handled themselves with such grace and class in a male dominated environment. These women could hang with male rappers lyrically, but, unlike others who came after them, they did not have to sound like men, losing their femininity, or sound like men want women to sound (hyper sexual) in order to excel. Who can imagine calling either of these two women a "bitch," let alone hearing them use the term to refer to themselves?

Changing the dialect is a start to changing the accepted behaviors in a culture. But women must close the door completely. If it is okay for men to use the term "when we're playing" or for women to use the term to refer to other women, then, like the 'N' word, its negative impact and implications may go away for a short time, but will return after just a little while. Then the word will continue to live and the women to whom it is applied will have a hard time living at the higher ends of the hierarchy.

Referenced

[1] http://www.pbs.org/wgbh/amex/mlk/filmmore/pt.html (accessed 10/21/15)

[2] Judson L. Jeffries; *Huey P. Newton: The Radical Theorist*; University Press (2006)

[3] Bobby Seale; Seize the Time: The Story of the Black Panther Party and Huey P. Newton; (Black Classic Press,1996) p. 4

[4] DJ Spooky (Ed), Naeem Mahaiemon; "Fear of a Muslim Planet: The Islamic Roots of Hip Hop" *Sound Unbound: Sampling Digital Music and Culture* (MIT Press, 2008)

[5] W.E.B. DuBois; The Souls of Black Folk (New York: Gramercy, 1994) p. 38

[6] The Bible, John Ch 10, v. 18

[7] http://www.nbcnews.com/id/19680493/ns/us_news-life/t/naacp-delegates-bury-n-word-ceremony/#.Vif6jX6rS00 (accessed 8/14/15)

[8] http://www.mvpmovie.com/?BlackPanthers

[9] http://www.thecrimson.com/article/1972/10/10/black-movies-a-new-wave-of/ (accessed 8/24/15)

[10] H.R. Haldeman; The Haldaman Diaries: Inside the Nixon White House (Putnam's Sons, 1994)

[11] Michelle Alexander; *The New Jim Crow: Mass Incarceration in the Age of Color Blindness* (New York: The New Press, 2012) p. 83-84

[12] Heather Cox Richardson, *The Death of Reconstruction: Race, Labor, and Politics in the Post-Civil War North, 1865–1901* (Cambridge: Harvard University Press, 2001), p. 216.

[13] http://www.huffingtonpost.com/wendy-brandes/kept-outta-compton-nwas-a_b_8101462.html (accessed 9/2/15)

[14] https://www.youtube.com/watch?v=HWpF7jYT5dm (accessed 9/12/15)

[15] http://grantland.com/features/rakim-big-daddy-kane-hip-hop-icons/ (accessed 9/20/15)

[16] Brian Coleman; *Rakim Told Me: Wax Facts Straight from the Original Artists—The '80s* (Wax Facts Press, 2005)

17 https://www.youtube.com/watch?v=FFh4BW_V59M
(accessed 9/12/15)
18 https://www.youtube.com/watch?v=H1FqxcfnWi0
(accessed 7/03/15)
19 https://www.youtube.com/watch?v=7XxyatRdaa0
(accessed 10/02/11)
20 Phillip Jenkins; *The Next Christendom: The Coming of Global Christianity* (Oxford University Press, 2011) p. 21-28
21 https://www.youtube.com/watch?v=gj6lM_ndkA0
(accessed 4/15/2015)
22 DJ Spooky (Ed), Naeem Mahaiemon; "Fear of a Muslim Planet: The Islamic Roots of Hip Hop" *Sound Unbound: Sampling Digital Music and Culture* (MIT Press, 2008)
23 ibid
24 Mark A. Noll; America's God: From Johnathan Edwards to Abraham Lincoln (Oxford University Press, 2005) p. 421
25 Ibid p. 420
26 James H. Cone, Gayraud S. Wilmore; *Black Theology: A Documentary History Vol 1* (Orbis: New York 1993) p. 66-67
27 Ibid p. 67
28 Ibid
29 Ibid p 70-71
30 Rufus Burrow Jr.; *James H. Cone and Black Liberation Theology*; (McFarland: Jefferson 1994) p. 14
31 DJ Spooky (Ed), Naeem Mahaiemon; "Fear of a Muslim Planet: The Islamic Roots of Hip Hop" *Sound Unbound: Sampling Digital Music and Culture* (MIT Press, 2008)
32 http://www.complex.com/music/2012/02/too-short-breaks-down-his-25-most-essential-songs/ (accessed 10/22/2015)
33 James H. Cone, The Cross and the Lynching Tree .... P 17
34 https://www.youtube.com/watch?v=bJlmDe9rWA8
(accessed 10/22/2015)

Made in the USA
Charleston, SC
24 February 2016